W9-CCY-122
Mrs. Pearlmutter

HOW THE JEWISH PEOPLE GREW UP

THE PUBLICATION OF THIS VOLUME WAS MADE POSSIBLE BY THE ESTABLISHMENT OF A FUND FOR THE PUBLICATION OF JEWISH RELIGIOUS SCHOOL LITERATURE

BY

THE NATIONAL FEDERATION OF TEMPLE SISTERHOODS

HOW THE JEWISH PEOPLE GREW UP

BY

MORDECAI I. SOLOFF

Educational Director of Temple Beth-El, Providence, R. I., Author of, When the Jewish People Was Young

Illustrated by LOUIS KABRIN

THE UNION
OF AMERICAN HEBREW CONGREGATIONS
NEW YORK, 1936

UNION GRADED SERIES

EDITED BY

EMANUEL GAMORAN, PH.D., *Director of Education*
Union of American Hebrew Congregations

Fifteenth Printing, 1957

PRINTED IN THE UNITED STATES OF AMERICA

55

TO

MY WIFE AND CO-WORKER

IN JEWISH EDUCATION

EVE LEE

Editor's Introduction

Jewish history is the most important subject taught in the Jewish religious school, as may be judged from the amount of time given to it in most of our schools. Most of the textbooks now available for teaching Jewish history are for older pupils; since there is a manifest need for a new series of books on Jewish history beyond biblical and post-biblical stories to meet the needs of younger children, the author, Mordecai I. Soloff, has prepared a course in Jewish history for the intermediate grades, namely, grades four, five, and six.

How the Jewish People Grew Up is the second in this series; it is a sequel to the previously published textbook, *When the Jewish People Was Young*. The present volume was first tried out in the Jewish schools of New York City, under the auspices of the New York Committee for School Extension, of which the late Rabbi Jacob B. Pollak was director. Several experimental editions in mimeographed form were published. On the basis of experimentation and in accordance with the suggestions of a number of readers the whole work has been thoroughly revised.

The teaching procedure is the so-called supervised study method. By means of a simplified "laboratory" procedure it provides for a period of supervised study of the text by all the pupils, as well as for a series of related readings and activities intended for the brighter pupils. For this reason, both a teacher's book and a pupil's workbook have been prepared. The present text is intended for the fifth grade of the Jewish religious school, that is, for children who are approximately ten years old.

The beautiful illustrations were drawn by Louis Kabrin, a talented young Jewish artist of Cincinnati.

We trust this book will prove a welcome addition to the textbook literature which the Commission on Jewish Education, through the Union of American Hebrew Congregations, is making available for the Jewish religious school.

EMANUEL GAMORAN

Acknowledgments

The original manuscript of "How the Jewish People Grew Up" was prepared in 1930 at the suggestion of Rabbi Jacob B. Pollak of blessed memory. He read and recommended improvements in content and style. He made available a person to type and illustrate the material and finally had the book mimeographed. The author cherishes the memory of Rabbi Pollak for his help, continuous encouragement, and many acts of friendship.

For six years, schools throughout the country, have been using this book in mimeographed form. Many detailed suggestions were brought to the attention of the author during that period of experimentation and all practical suggestions were incorporated in the present edition. The entire book was rewritten. Its length was slightly reduced by the omission of several chapters and the facts presented are in accordance with some of the latest interpretations of the periods discussed.

To all who were kind enough to offer suggestions, the author is very grateful. He is particularly indebted to Dr. Emanuel Gamoran, Educational Director of the Commission on Jewish Education, Dr. Henry Englander, Dr. Solomon A. Fineberg and Dr. William Rosenau of the Commission on Jewish Education, Rabbi William G. Braude of Temple Beth-El, Providence, and Dr. Leo L. Honor, Director of the Board of Jewish Education in Chicago, for the many constructive criticisms in content, interpretation of facts, and style.

The writer also wishes to thank Mrs. M. Myer Singer for her careful revision of style.

How the Jewish People Grew Up deals with the history of the Jewish People from the time of the Return to Palestine in 536 B.C.E. to their exile from Spain in 1492. Like the preceding volume, *When the Jewish People Was Young,* it is a continuous story of the adventures of the Jewish people.

M. I. S.

Providence, R. I., 1936

Table of Contents

List of Illustrations

List of Maps

HOW THE JEWISH PEOPLE GREW UP

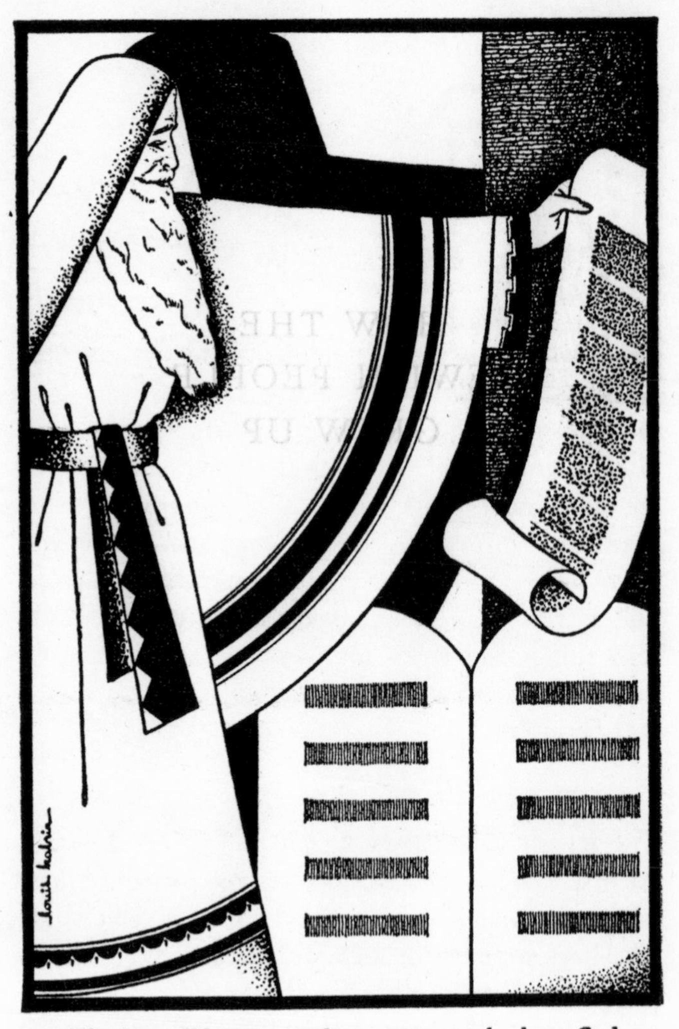

The Jews did not even know very much about God until Moses taught them, . . .

How Did the Jewish People Grow Up?

As the years go by, you grow taller and heavier, and you become older and wiser. You learn how to do many things. As a little child, you needed help in such simple acts as eating and walking; now you are old enough to read books and write letters. In the coming years, you will change even more. You will grow bigger and stronger in body; your knowledge will increase and so will your ability to understand why things happen as they do. Instead of receiving help from others, you will be able to *give* help, for you will be grown up.

I. WHEN THE JEWISH PEOPLE WAS STILL YOUNG

The Jewish people grew up just as you are growing. At first, some four thousand years ago, when the Jewish people was young, it was very small and weak. The Jews were few in number, and had little knowledge of how to provide for their needs. They were able to get food, make clothes and tents, ride camels and donkeys, and bring sacrifices to their God. But they had not yet learned how to grow grain, fruit, or vegetables. They were about a thousand years old, and had lived in Palestine for some time, before they knew anything about farming.

The Jews did not even know very much about God until Moses taught them; and that was hundreds of years after Abraham had lived. Even then, the Jews did not understand what God expected of them. The great prophets who appeared long after the death of Moses, tried to teach them how God wanted them to live. And even in the days of the prophets, when the Jewish people was about 1500 years old, most of the Jews still believed that they could worship God by merely bringing Him sacrifices. They did not realize that they had to be honest, kind, and thoughtful if they wished to be true servants of God.

The holy books which teach us to live as good Jews, were not yet in existence. The Bible was not known, and other books which Jews now hold dear, such as the Talmud and the Prayerbook, had not been written. Indeed, very few Jews knew how to read at all in those early days. The Jewish people was young, then.

Please open your Workbook to Chapter 1 entitled: "How Did the Jewish People Grow Up?" Under Topic I, you will find a few easy questions. When you finish with the questions listed under the first topic, turn back to this textbook and continue your reading.

II. WHEN THE JEWISH PEOPLE GREW UP

But as time passed, the Jewish people grew bigger and stronger and wiser. During the 4000 years since Abraham, the number of Jews has increased to more than sixteen million men, women, and children. They have learned to earn a living by doing handwork and manufacturing, or by engaging in business or the professions. They have also learned the way to serve God. Instead of bringing Him sacrifices they try to be honest, kind, and thoughtful of others.

It is clear that, as they grew in strength and knowledge, the Jews changed a great deal. But we must not imagine that these changes all happened at one time. No indeed! They came about, little by little. At first, Jews worshipped God by bringing Him sacrifices. Later, they recited prayers while the Kohanim offered up the sacrifices. Now, we offer up no sacrifices; we recite prayers. In earning a living, long ago, most Jews were shepherds. Later they turned to farming. Now, the majority of the Jews live in cities and are neither shepherds nor farmers, but hand workers, business men, or in the professions.

How the Jewish people grew to be what it now is, makes an interesting story. If you study your lessons carefully, you will understand just what happened to our people. You will be told how they grew in number, strength, and wisdom. You will learn how the Bible was arranged, how the Talmud was compiled, and how a number of other important books came into being. You will find out also how the Jews were finally driven out of Palestine and scattered over the face of the earth. You will see how they changed their occupations to suit their new homes and how they changed their laws, customs, and ways of living. You

Later, they recited prayers. . . .

will then have a better understanding of the people to which you belong.

Now stop your reading for a moment and turn once more to your Workbook. Answer the questions under Topic II of this chapter.

III. HOW TO LEARN YOUR LESSON

The method of study will probably be familiar to you. Nevertheless, it will be wise for you to take note of these directions.

1. Read the textbook as rapidly as possible. Before you go far, you will find a note directing you to answer some questions in your Workbook. Turn at once to the proper place in your Workbook and write your answers. Should any question be too hard for you, re-read the part you read before. If you still do not know the answer, ask your teacher to help you. As soon as you finish writing the answers, go back to your textbook, read the next topic, and answer the questions on the second topic. Continue reading your textbook and writing in your Workbook by turns until you finish the chapter.

2. If you finish studying the chapter quickly enough, you will be given an opportunity to read one of several other books. Which books to read and what stories to choose, will be pointed out at the end of each chapter. This additional reading will be interesting, and will help you understand and remember what you have just studied in your history book.

3. In case the class is asked to stop work before you

finish all the reading and writing, you may complete the work at home.

4. During the last part of the period you will be allowed to have some interesting activity, such as making up a playlet based on the lesson, drawing or coloring pictures, conducting a class discussion or watching a slide show.

5. For each chapter you read in class, there is a Homework-Test in your Workbook. Take the test any time before you return to class. The entire Homework-Test can be finished in a very short time. Be sure it is correct before you turn it in.

For additional suggestions concerning work at home, and for information on the system used in marking your work, see the directions at the beginning of your Workbook.

6. The most important point to remember is that *you* are to do the work and *you* are to learn the lesson. Your teacher and your parents may help you, but no one may do the work for you.

Answer the questions under Topic III.

ADDITIONAL READING

If you finish reading this chapter and answering the questions in the Workbook before the teacher gives you any other work, you may use the next few minutes to get acquainted with some other books which you will find interesting. The first book is *The Unconquered,* written by Joseph Gaer, the same man who wrote *The Burning Bush.* Read one of the stories.

You will find it most enjoyable. Another book is Rose Lurie's, *The Great March*. It is full of dramatic stories of great interest. Read one of them and see for yourself.

SOMETHING TO THINK ABOUT

1. What do we mean when we say: "The Jewish people grew up"?
2. What is a "holy" book?

How Did the Jews Begin to Rebuild Palestine?

You have already learned what happened when the Jewish people was young. To help you understand this year's work, how the Jewish people grew up, we will summarize the story very briefly.

I. EARLY JEWISH HISTORY

The Jewish people was born 4000 years ago when Abraham left his Aramean home, crossed the Euphrates River, and entered Palestine. At that time, the Jews were an unimportant, wandering tribe of shepherds. Later they settled in Palestine, became farmers and learned about God from their prophets, Kohanim, and Levites.

Unfortunately, Assyria destroyed Israel. Later Babylonia did the same to Judah. They killed many Jews, drove their leaders into exile, and burnt the Temple. But 50 years after Jerusalem had been destroyed, Cyrus, the King of Persia and conqueror of Babylonia, permitted the Jews to return to Palestine and rebuild their land.

And return they did. With songs on their lips and joy in their hearts, Jews, by the thousands, left the lands of their exile and came back to the land of their dreams—Palestine.

Now turn to Chapter 2 in your Workbook, and answer the questions under Topic I.

II. THE HARDSHIPS FACING THE RETURNED EXILES

But rebuilding the land proved more difficult than they had expected. When the exiles finally reached Jerusalem, they built a new altar on top of Mt. Zion where their Temple had once stood. The Kohanim offered sacrifices, while the others watched them respectfully. When the brief service was over, the people scattered in search of homes.

Many of the former exiles returned to the villages in which they or their fathers had lived before, while the majority settled in Jerusalem or near-by. But getting comfortably settled was a difficult matter. There were very few good homes into which they could move at once. The Babylonian soldiers had destroyed most of the city when they had finally succeeded in capturing it, and the few houses left standing were occupied by those Jews who had remained. Just a few wealthy families were able to buy or rent good homes; the large majority were forced to live for some time in tents, in hastily built shacks, or in the open. Getting food was not much easier. The returned exiles had not as yet raised any grain or vegetables in their own fields, and did not want to kill their sheep and cattle for food. Thus they were forced to buy food from those Jews who had not gone

. . . with songs on their lips, Jews came back to the land of their dreams—Palestine.

into exile and from merchants who occasionally came into the city. The poorer among the returned exiles found food expensive and suffered from hunger.

But the hardest blow to the returned exiles was the discovery that most of their good fields and homes outside of Jerusalem were in the hands of strangers. Moabites, Ammonites, Philistines, and others had taken possession of some of the best sections of the country. Only a well trained army could have driven these people out of the land. The Jews had no army, so they took what land was left and set to work rebuilding homes and plowing fields.

Before long, many families discovered that their fields did not produce enough food. Some other way of earning a livelihood had to be found. A number of men then hired themselves out as laborers, while a few sold themselves as slaves to their wealthier brethren. Everyone hoped that within a few years, the fields would produce more food, the merchants would earn more money, and all would be able to live more comfortably.

Unfortunately, a number of years passed without improvement. Sometimes locusts would come and eat up the little food that had been raised in the fields. Sometimes robbers carried off the food and goods that had been stored up. Tax collectors for the Persian government always came to get the portion of food and goods due the ruler; and officers also came very often to get men for the Persian army.

Answer the questions under Topic II.

III. WHAT HELPED OUR ANCESTORS?

These continued hardships made the returned exiles unhappy and slowed down the work of rebuilding their homes, the roads and the cities. Many became discouraged and returned to Babylonia or went to some other land that seemed more promising. But the majority did not lose heart. They continued their efforts to rebuild the land. There were two reasons for this. First, they were happy to live in Palestine, the holy land. Secondly, Jews kept coming from Babylonia bringing food, clothing, and money. This encouraged them to stay on and rebuild the Temple, and continue to worship God as their ancestors had done.

For years, however, the Jews in Palestine were so occupied with their troubles that even the Temple remained unbuilt. Fully twenty years passed before the House of God was finally erected; and then only because of the urging of two great prophets—Haggai and Zechariah. These prophets called upon their fellow-Jews to rebuild the Temple as rapidly as possible so that they might again worship God in a holy place. The prophets declared that God would surely help them if they would obey His commandments.

Inspired by the words of Haggai and Zechariah, the Jews set earnestly to work, rebuilding the Temple. All the Jews in Jerusalem and the villages near-by were eager to help. Trees were cut down, stones were gathered, and mortar was prepared. Under the guidance of some of the older men who had seen the

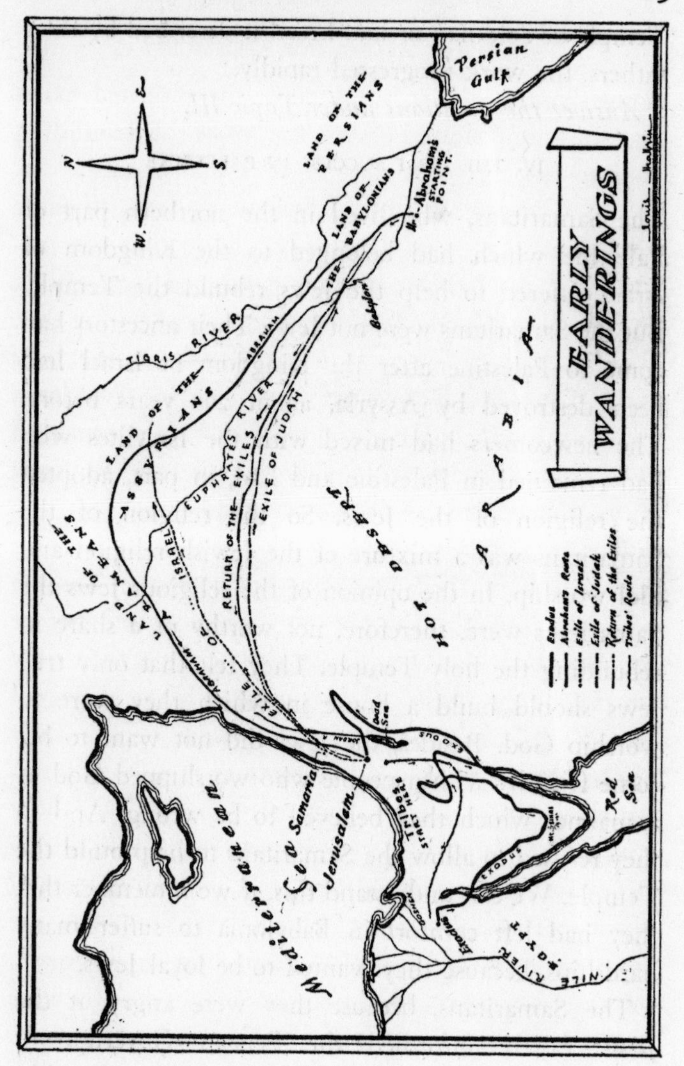
EARLY WANDERINGS
Persian Gulf
LAND OF THE PERSIANS
THE LAND OF BABYLONIANS
Ur. Abraham's STARTING POINT.
Babylon
TIGRIS RIVER
ABRAHAM
LAND OF THE ASSYRIANS
EUPHRATES RIVER
EXILE OF JUDAH
RETURN OF THE EXILES
ISRAEL
EXILE OF
LAND OF ABRAHAM
THE LAND OF
DESERT
ARABIA
Mediterranean Sea
Samaria
Jerusalem
Dead Sea
EXODUS
Tribes START HERE
Red Sea
NILE RIVER
EGYPT
Exodus
Abraham's Route
Exile of Israel
Exile of Judah
Return of the Exiles
Tribes' Route
N
S
W
E

Temple of Solomon or had heard it described by their fathers, the work progressed rapidly.

Answer the questions under Topic III.

IV. THE FIRST SUCCESS IN PALESTINE

The Samaritans, who lived in the northern part of Palestine which had belonged to the Kingdom of Israel, offered to help the Jews rebuild the Temple. But the Samaritans were not Jews. Their ancestors had come to Palestine after the Kingdom of Israel had been destroyed by Assyria, about 200 years before. The newcomers had mixed with the Israelites who had remained in Palestine and had, in part, adopted the religion of the Jews. So the religion of the Samaritans was a mixture of the Jewish religion and idol worship. In the opinion of the religious Jews the Samaritans were, therefore, not worthy of a share in rebuilding the holy Temple. They felt that only true Jews should build a house in which they were to worship God. Besides, the Jews did not want to become friendly with a people who worshipped God in a manner which they believed to be wrong. And so they refused to allow the Samaritans to help build the Temple. We can understand this, if we remember that they had left comfort in Babylonia to suffer many hardships, because they wanted to be loyal Jews.

The Samaritans, because they were angry at the Jews, falsely informed the Persian Governor of Palestine that the Jews were building a Temple without the permission of his government. The governor immediately ordered the Jews to cease work. It took much precious time to prove that the Jews had received permission from the former king, Cyrus. Only when the Persian governor was convinced that the Jews had this right, did he permit them to complete the Temple. Great was their joy at this news.

In the year 516 before the common era, which you know was over 2450 years ago, the Jews held a great celebration in honor of the new Temple. The Kohanim, assisted by the Levites, brought sacrifices with songs and rejoicing. Among those present, there were only a few who could recall the glories of Solomon's Temple. They wept because the new Temple was not as beautiful as the old; yet the second Temple was destined to stand for more than 200 years longer than the first.

The completion of the Second Temple by the returned exiles, was the first important step in the rebuilding of Palestine. But it was only a beginning. Even Jerusalem was still full of tumble-down houses. Imagine, therefore, how little had been done to rebuild the other cities and villages. The rebuilding of the land was to be a long and difficult task.

Answer the questions under Topic IV.

ADDITIONAL READING

The Bible. Most of what we know about the Jews living in Palestine 2400 years ago, we learned by reading the books of Ezra and Nehemiah found in the Bible on pages 1027–1057.

In our lesson, we also mentioned the prophets Haggai and Zechariah. Their prophecies are written in our Bible. You can find these on pages 757–770.

When you get home, try reading these books with your parents. You will find them very interesting.

Right now, look up the following verses. They will give you the answers to the questions that precede them.

Why did the Jews return to Palestine? Page 1027, Book of Ezra, Chap. 1, verse 5.

How many Jews went back to Palestine? Page 1029, Book of Ezra, Chap. 2, verse 64.

What difficulty arose with the Samaritans? Page 1030, Book of Ezra, Chap. 4, verses 1–6.

What did the Persian king Darius permit the Jews to do? Page 1033, Book of Ezra, Chap. 6, verse 7.

The Unconquered. What kind of people were the Persian rulers? The story "The Triumph of Truth," beginning on page 21, will tell you. If you want a good laugh, read the first two stories also.

The Great March. How the Jews returned from Babylonia to Judea and rebuilt the Temple is told on pages 1–9. Read that story. You will like it.

SOMETHING TO THINK ABOUT

1. When the first exiles finally returned to Palestine, they were greatly disappointed. Why?
2. Were the Jews wise in refusing to accept the help of the Samaritans? Why?

What Difficulties Faced the Returned Exiles?

IT WAS a great joy to see the Temple rebuilt, seventy years after the Babylonians had destroyed it. Yet the people who had returned from Babylonia were not happy. There were three important difficulties which constantly worried them.

1. They were frequently attacked and robbed.
2. It was hard for them to earn a living, even during times of peace.
3. They were unable to practice their religion properly.

1. WHY WERE JEWS OFTEN ATTACKED IN PALESTINE?

The three reasons for the unhappiness of our people are hard for us to understand. When we learn that the people were frequently attacked and robbed, we wonder: Who attacked and robbed the Jews? Why did they do it? Why did the policemen and judges allow such things to happen? Where were the soldiers and their officers? What was the leader of the Jewish people doing to stop the attacks?

To answer these questions, we must remember that these events took place more than 2400 years ago. At that time, there lived in Palestine many kinds of people besides Jews. There were, you recall, Moabites, Ammonites, Philistines, Samaritans, and others that are not so well-known.

When the Jews who owned the land came back to Palestine, some of the non-Jews had to leave their homes there and go elsewhere. This made them angry and they attacked the Jews whenever they could. Others robbed the Jews simply because they wanted their property. And some of the Samaritans fell upon the Jews in revenge for not being allowed to help rebuild the Temple.

These unjust attacks continued for many years, because the Jews were unable to protect themselves properly. They had no policemen to watch their homes, nor did they have an army to protect their cities and villages. The rich people engaged servants to guard their families, their homes, and their property. The poor people had to defend themselves as best as they could, or, when attacked, depend upon the help of their neighbors.

The robbers might have completely destroyed the Jews, had not the Persian governor who lived many miles from Jerusalem occasionally sent troops to drive them off. The Persian governor protected the people because the land belonged to Persia and those who lived there paid taxes to the Persian ruler, and supplied young men for his army.

In your Workbook you may now answer the questions under Topic I of Chapter 3.

The Jews . . . sent him gifts for the temple and money for the support of poor Jews.

II. HOW WAS PEACE KEPT AMONG THE JEWS?

Besides suffering from other peoples, the Jews at times quarreled with one another over business, religious, or family affairs. Such fights were usually settled by the head of the Temple, the chief Kohen, who bore the honored title of "Kohen Gadol" (the highest Kohen, or High Priest). The Kohen Gadol was recognized as the leader of the Jews because:

1. He was the Kohen in charge of the Temple, and directed the people in the worship of God. Since nothing was so important to the Jews as the proper service of God, the Kohen Gadol was the most respected man among them.

2. The Kohen Gadol was learned in Jewish law. He read many of the holy books and knew them well. He was thus able to settle disputes in accordance with the Law of God.

Even outside of Palestine the Kohen Gadol was recognized as the Jewish leader. The Jews who lived in Babylonia, Egypt, and other lands sent him gifts for the Temple and money for the support of poor Jews. The Persian governor, too, looked upon the Kohen Gadol as the head of the Jews in Palestine and consulted with him on all matters concerning them.

Unfortunately the Kohen Gadol had no army with which to defend his people against attacks and robberies. The Persian soldiers were usually too far away, and the Jews alone were not strong enough.

As a result, robbery and murder were often committed and seldom punished.

Answer the questions under Topic II.

III. WHAT DISCOURAGED THE RETURNED EXILES?

But even worse hardships faced the Jews in Palestine. Many poor people had such small and rocky fields that they could barely raise enough food for their families. Part of this small quantity, they had to give to the Persian governor in payment of taxes. Part of it went to the Kohanim serving in the Temple. When a year came during which there was too much or too little rain, the poor farmers had to borrow from the rich. When such a year was followed by another during which locusts came and ate the crops, many of the farmers sold themselves as slaves, to pay their debts.

But perhaps the worst discouragement was in connection with the worship of their God. They or their parents had broken up their homes in Babylonia, left their friends, and gone on the long and difficult journey to Palestine in order to serve God in His holy city, Jerusalem. What did they find? Twenty years had passed before they had been able to rebuild even the Temple. And after it had been completed, at the urging of Haggai and Zechariah, the farmers were too poor to pay for its upkeep. As a result, the Kohanim were forced to go elsewhere to find means of support, leaving the Temple bare, and hardly fit for worship. Moreover, it was hard to observe the

Sabbath properly. Strangers disturbed this holy day by selling their goods, and some of the Jews cared so little about the Sabbath that they and their servants worked as usual on that day. To make matters worse, many Jews married non-Jewish women. These mothers did not teach their children the Jewish religion and let them grow up without any knowledge of God and His commandments.

The attacks on their homes, the poverty of the farmers, and the difficulty of observing their religion in Palestine made the Jews very unhappy.

For many years they worked with might and main, but without much success. The men and women who first came to Palestine in the days of Cyrus, died. Their children grew old. But still there was no sign of improvement. To many people it seemed as if the Jews would either have to leave Palestine or give up their Judaism. The task of rebuilding the land was altogether neglected.

Answer the questions under Topic III.

ADDITIONAL READING

The Bible. Who were some of those who attacked the Jews?

In the Book of Zechariah, Chapter 9, verse 5, page 764, you will find the names of the cities belonging to the Philistines.

How the Jews respected their Kohen Gadol is described in Zechariah, Chapter 6, verse 11, page 762.

How poor the Jews became because of high taxes,

we can judge by their bringing blind, lame, and sick animals as sacrifices. The Prophet Malachi was angry at the Jews for doing this. Read his own words on page 771, Book of Malachi, Chapter 1, verse 8.

The Book of Nehemiah, Chapter 5, verses 2, 3, 4, pages 1044, tells of the poverty of those Jews.

Why the Kohanim and Levites left the Temple is told in the Book of Nehemiah, Chapter 13, verse 10, page 1056.

SOMETHING TO THINK ABOUT

1. Why did not the Jews organize an army to drive out those who attacked them?
2. Why was the Kohen Gadol considered a good ruler?
3. Was it as easy to be a good Jew in Babylonia as in Palestine?

Chapter 4

How Did the Exiles Overcome Their Difficulties?

FOR almost a hundred years, the Jews had suffered attacks by robbers, poverty, and neglect of their religion, before there came a change for the better. This happened with the arrival in Palestine, 2400 years ago, of Ezra the Sofer (the Scribe). (The title "Sofer" means "one who writes." It was given to scholars who wrote copies of our holy books.)

I. HOW EZRA TRIED TO HELP

When Ezra the Sofer who lived in Babylonia, made known his intention of going to Jerusalem, many Persian Jews decided to accompany him. Others, who stayed behind, gave him gifts for the Jews in Palestine. After a journey of several months, Ezra the Sofer arrived in Jerusalem with 1500 followers.

The Sofer delivered the gifts and settled down in his new home. It was not long before he discovered that most of the Jews did not know the contents of the holy books, and that only a few observed the laws of the Jewish people.

This discovery was a bitter disappointment to Ezra.

Ezra called a meeting of the heads of the families.

What grieved him most, was the fact that many Jews had not taught their children the Jewish laws and customs. Many of the young people did not even know the Hebrew language.

Ezra called a meeting of the heads of the families. It was held in the Temple. When the people were assembled, Ezra spoke to them with bowed head, and aching heart. There were tears in his eyes. The old Sofer told his listeners that they had done wrong in failing to carry out the commandments of God. He was especially sad because some of them had married foreign women and allowed their children to grow up without knowledge of how Jews should live. The people listened very attentively. They realized that many of the non-Jewish women worshipped idols and taught their children to do likewise. They understood also that these women might lead them all away from the worship of God and thus bring to an end the life of the Jewish people. They therefore promised to send away their foreign wives immediately. Furthermore, they decided to study the holy books and learn them well.

Some people sent the foreign women away as they had promised. It was heart-breaking for them to do so; yet they realized that it was the only way possible to save the Jewish people from becoming idol-worshippers like their neighbors. But those who had given their daughters in marriage to the Jews, did not understand why the men had suddenly sent the women away. They were insulted at the way the Jews had treated their daughters. In revenge, they attacked the Jews, and destroyed the homes of many. As a result the Jews were poorer than before. More of them were forced to borrow money for food and clothing, and more had to sell themselves and their children into slavery in order to pay their debts. Once again a feeling of despair came over the people.

In your Workbook, answer the questions to Topic I of Chapter 4.

II. WHAT NEHEMIAH LEARNED

But God would not let His people die. He sent them help from far-off Persia. In that country, there lived a Jew by the name of Nehemiah, who was a high officer in the court of the Persian king. Nehemiah had been hearing reports of what had happened in Palestine, and knew how unhappy the Jews there were. He had rejoiced when he had heard of Ezra's arrival in Palestine and sorrowed at the news of how the Jews suffered at the hands of their neighbors. One day the king noticed that Nehemiah was very unhappy and asked him why. Nehemiah explained that he had received sad news from Palestine: that the Jews there were in great trouble, and needed help. The king, thereupon, appointed Nehemiah governor of Palestine. Nehemiah was overjoyed. He thanked the king and immediately departed. That was in 445 B.C.E.

Nehemiah did not immediately announce that he was the governor. He came to Jerusalem so quietly that no one realized who he was. At night, riding on a horse, he secretly inspected the wall around Jerusalem. He found that it was badly broken in many places and that the gates had been burned. Many sections of the city were deserted, and the roads were in bad shape. The Temple itself seemed empty and looked as if it needed to be cleaned and repaired.

Answer the questions under Topic II.

III. HOW JERUSALEM WAS MADE SAFE

Nehemiah now knew what had to be done. He showed the letters of the king to the Persian officers, to the Kohen Gadol, and to the other Jewish leaders to prove that he was governor of Palestine. At once, Nehemiah was recognized as the ruler of the Jews. His first undertaking was the erection of a wall around Jerusalem. He asked every man to give part of his time to the building of the wall. The people were only too glad to help. Quickly they set to work. When their enemies, the Samaritans, heard what Nehemiah was doing they tried to stop him by spreading a rumor that he was planning to rebel against the king. However, neither Nehemiah nor anybody else paid any attention to these reports, for the governor had the written permission of the Persian king to do whatever he wished. When the Samaritans found that their reports did not stop the work on the wall, they tried to attack the men working on it. But Nehemiah was ready for them. He had given the workmen swords in addition to their tools, and when the time came, the men used their weapons as well as their tools. As a result, it

At night, riding on a horse, he secretly inspected the wall around Jerusalem.

took only two months to complete the wall about Jerusalem.

The people living inside the city were now safe from the attacks of robbers. However, there were not enough people living in the city of Jerusalem to defend it in case of attack by an army. Nehemiah, therefore, decided to increase the number of Jews in the city by inviting those who lived in the villages near-by to come to Jerusalem. Being both rich and generous, Nehemiah built houses for those who did not have enough money to build their own. He made loans to those in need of money. He did not even collect taxes with which to pay his salary as governor. In this way he succeeded in persuading a large number of Jews to come and live in Jerusalem. The Jews now felt safe.

Nehemiah knew that many Jews were heavily in debt to the richer Jews, that some of them had given up their homes and fields, and that a number of them had sold their children or themselves as slaves in payment of debts. Nehemiah knew that such people could never be happy. He, therefore, called together the rich men and asked them to release the Jews from paying back the money they had borrowed. He urged them also to return the fields which they had taken and to free those Jews who had become their slaves. Because everybody respected Nehemiah for helping all the Jews living in Palestine, the rich did as Nehemiah had asked them.

Great was the rejoicing that followed the announcement that the Jewish slaves were free, that the money which the poor owed to the rich need not be repaid, and that the fields, taken from the poor, would be returned. At last each man felt able to earn a living for his family.

Answer the questions under Topic III.

IV. HOW THE PEOPLE WERE TAUGHT TO PRACTICE THEIR RELIGION

Nehemiah now set about the task of helping the Jews go back to the proper service of God. The governor caused a law to be passed, requiring all Jews to pay taxes for the support of the Kohanim and Levites serving in the Temple. He appointed officers to collect these taxes and give the money and the grain to the Kohanim and Levites working in the Temple. The Jews living outside of Palestine—in Babylonia, Egypt, and elsewhere—also felt it their duty to pay taxes for the Temple. As a result the Kohanim and the Levites could now return to the Temple and take care of it.

Some time later, the Kohen Gadol found that the money from the collections in Palestine and the gifts from Jews living outside of Palestine amounted to so much that he could pay the Kohanim and Levites, buy everything he needed for the Temple, make all the necessary repairs on the building and furnishings, help the poor, and still save some of it for a time when it would be needed. The troubles of the Kohanim thus came to an end, and the Temple was made fit to serve as the House of God.

Nehemiah was now ready for his most important

task; helping the Jews learn and obey the laws of God. In this undertaking, Ezra the Sofer proved himself a great leader. Being, by far, the most learned man in the community, the Sofer taught the Kohanim and Levites the contents of the books which the Jews considered holy. Just before the Sukkot Festival when a large number of Jews came to Jerusalem, Ezra stood on a wooden pulpit built in the market place and read from one of the holy books some of the laws dealing with Sukkot. Several Levites explained the meaning of what was read. The people were happy to learn the contents of the holy book and gladly followed the instructions. Thereafter, parts of the holy books were read on other festive occasions. As the years went by, it became customary to read these books on all market and festival days. To this day, Jews assemble in the synagogues to hear parts of the Bible read every Sabbath, Monday, and Thursday. As time passed, more and more people learned the laws and followed them. Finally, Nehemiah persuaded the Jews to stop working on the Sabbath, and ordered the gates of Jerusalem to be locked on that day so that no outsiders should come in to disturb the peace of the Sabbath. And so the Jews were finally enabled to serve God and live according to His laws.

For a number of years, our people were free to devote their energies toward the rebuilding of the land, and realizing the dreams of their fathers who had been exiles in Babylon.

Answer the questions to Topic IV.

ADDITIONAL READING

The Bible. We have two books in the Bible that bear the names of Ezra the Sofer, and Nehemiah the Governor. In these two books, we can find most of the information that we now have about these men and the people who lived at that time. It would be fine to read their own stories in the language which they themselves used—mostly Hebrew and a little Aramaic. However, for the present we must be satisfied with reading an English translation. The Book of Ezra is found in your Bible on pages 1027–1039, and the Book of Nehemiah on pages 1039–1057.

Why did Ezra feel unhappy when he arrived in Palestine? Page 1037, Book of Ezra, Chapter 9, verses 2–3.

What did Ezra say to the people? Page 1037, Book of Ezra, Chap. 9, verses 4, 5, 6, and 12.

Why was Nehemiah sad when he heard what was happening in Palestine? Page 1039, Book of Nehemiah, Chap. 1, verses 1–4.

What position did Nehemiah hold in Persia? Page 1040, Book of Nehemiah, Chap. 1, verse 11.

NOTE: A cupbearer in those days was one of the highest officers, because the king was afraid that an ordinary servant might put poison in his wine.

How did Nehemiah happen to be appointed governor of Palestine? Page 1040, Book of Nehemiah, Chapter 2, verses 2–8.

How did Nehemiah find out about the situation in Jerusalem? Page 1041, Nehemiah, Chap. 2, verses 11–13.

What did Nehemiah do to make Jerusalem safe? Page 1043, Book of Nehemiah, Chap. 3, verse 38.

How did the enemies of the Jews feel when they saw the walls being built? Page 1043, Book of Nehemiah, Chap. 4, verses 1–2.

What did Nehemiah do to help the poor? Page 1044, Book of Nehemiah, Chap. 5, verses 11–12.

How did Ezra teach the Jews to know the Torah? Page 1048, Book of Nehemiah, Chap. 8, verses 2–3.

How did Nehemiah arrange the taxes for the Temple? Page 1056, Book of Nehemiah, Chap. 13, verses 12–13.

Did the Jews keep the Sabbath? Page 1056, Book of Nehemiah, Chap. 13, verses 15–16.

What did Nehemiah do to make the Jews keep the Sabbath? Page 1056, Book of Nehemiah, Chap. 13, verse 19.

What did Nehemiah demand of those who married foreign women? Page 1057, Book of Nehemiah, Chap. 13, verse 25.

The Unconquered. There are two stories you will enjoy reading:

1. "Cup-Bearer to the King," beginning on page 43.
2. "The Bad Samaritan," beginning on page 51.

SOMETHING TO THINK ABOUT

1. Many people think Ezra the Sofer helped the Jews more than Nehemiah the Governor. Do you agree with them? Why?
2. Nowadays, we do not build walls around cities.

Why was it necessary to build a wall in the days of Ezra and Nehemiah?

3. Nowadays Kohanim are of little importance to Jews. Yet Nehemiah considered them so important that he taxed the Jewish people to support them. Was he right? Why?

What Did the Returned Exiles Accomplish?

THE assistance of Ezra and Nehemiah enabled the Jews in Palestine to live more peacefully and happily. Ezra and Nehemiah also taught them to observe the Sabbath and holy days and to worship God.

But many Jews were still ignorant of some of the most important Jewish laws. This was not due to lack of desire to learn. They had no system of schools, nor any book, like the Bible, to help them live as Jews. How did the Jews overcome these difficulties? What did they accomplish?

I. WHAT WAS THE "ANSHE KENESET HA-GEDOLAH"?

In the days of Ezra and Nehemiah (2400 years ago), the entire book we now call the Bible, from which the Jewish people still learns much of its religion, was not yet in existence. Only parts of it had been written at that time and these parts were on separate scrolls. Often the wording in two scrolls containing the same story was different. In addition, most Jews had no copies at all, and only a few of them had enough learning to understand the laws written on the scrolls which they possessed. Therefore, the Jews could know and follow only those laws which they learned while visiting a local synagogue or the Temple in Jerusalem. Ezra the Sofer realized that the Jews would have to know God's laws well and follow them if they were to become His true servants.

Ezra discussed the matter with Nehemiah. Together they called a meeting of the most learned men in Jerusalem and explained to them the great necessity of teaching the people to know the laws according to which they must live. A society called the "Anshe Keneset Ha-gedolah"—men of the great assembly—was then formed, whose purpose it was to help the Jews live in accordance with the laws of God. The Anshe Keneset Ha-gedolah served the Jewish people for many years. At their head stood the Kohen Gadol, the holy man who spoke in the name of God. They met whenever the Kohen Gadol, who was also the Jewish ruler, wanted advice and help. One of their first tasks was to appoint judges who knew the Jewish laws well, and who would reach a decision only after considering all the arguments presented by both sides in a case. But the judges faced a serious difficulty. There was no set of laws recognized by all, to guide them. They had some scrolls on which ancient Jewish laws were written. But they did not know whether they had *all* the laws. They were not even certain that all the laws recorded in their scrolls were still to be followed. What could the judges do?

Answer the questions given under Topic I, Chapter 5 of your Workbook.

II. HOW WAS THE BIBLE MADE UP?

To provide a guide for the judges and the people, the Anshe Keneset Ha-gedolah collected copies of all books or scrolls that might be holy. They then examined each one carefully. Some of the books were not considered holy and were laid aside. Years later, some of these were found. Together with others, written at a later date, they formed a special collection, called Apocrypha. One of the most important of these is the Book of Maccabees, telling the story of Hanukkah. We shall study this event in a later chapter.

The books, considered holy were treated differently. They were first arranged in good order. Then the Anshe Keneset Ha-gedolah studied each one of them carefully. Over and over they studied the meaning of each chapter and verse in these books to make sure they were just right. Indeed, they studied every single word and letter! Mistakes were carefully corrected. Sentences which did not seem clear, were slightly changed, and chapters were often given introductory sentences, to make them easier for the reader to understand. Thus began the work of making the Bible—the set of books which has become the most famous ever written. It is so fine a piece of literature that it has been translated into hundreds of languages and studied by millions of people.

We Jews may well be proud of this accomplishment. You must understand that it took many years to complete the work. Indeed, the task lasted for several

They had some scrolls on which ancient Jewish laws were written.

hundred years. Ezra, Nehemiah, and the other members of the Anshe Keneset Ha-gedolah who began the work did not live to see its completion.

The Anshe Keneset Ha-gedolah worked steadily at the books, which, in part, make up our Bible. As soon as one of them was completed, Soferim were permitted to make copies on scrolls and sell them. Naturally, the judges, Kohanim, Levites, and other Jewish leaders secured them first. But even the farmers and laborers were eager to get the holy books, and ready to pay for them.

Answer the questions to Topic II.

III. HOW DID THE PEOPLE PAY?

Incidentally, you will be interested to know how the people who lived in Palestine some 2300 years ago paid for what they bought. There were three ways of paying. A few rich Jews had Persian coins. These people of course paid in money. But most of the Jews at that time had no money. They were farmers who had food which they raised on their farms, clothes from the wool or skins of the animals which they kept, and homes which they or the members of their family had built. When they needed something they could not make, they exchanged something they had for whatever they wanted.

Not all the Jews were farmers, however. Many of them were handworkers. They were able to build houses, make furniture, fashion tools, manufacture clothing, or do other useful work. Such people gave their labor in exchange for food and other things which they desired.

Handworkers and farmers were generally poor; most of them could not afford to buy all the books. But occasionally they did get one or two of the books, and gradually collected many if not all the books of the Bible that were available.

There was no need to get all the books at once. They were not bound together as they are at present. It was hardly possible to do so. The books of those days were in the form of scrolls like those you see in synagogue on Sabbath mornings. A set of books was too big and bulky for one to handle. You know how big the Sefer Torah is—and it contains only the first five books. Imagine then how big a scroll the Bible, which was later completed, would have made. True it is that some of the books are very small, but others are large, indeed, larger than any of the first five.

Answer the questions to Topic III.

IV. WHAT ARE THE CONTENTS OF THE BIBLE?

The books of the Bible were separated into three main divisions. The first group of books became known as the Torah—we sometimes call them The Five Books of Moses. These books are so well known, that you will no doubt be familiar with their names and perhaps even with their contents. They are: Genesis, Exodus, Leviticus, Numbers, Deuteronomy.

The second division, called Nebiim (prophets), contains twenty-one separate books. Many of these are named after prophets and heroes whose life and work you have already studied. Here are their names: Joshua, Judges (Do you remember Deborah? Gideon? Jephthah? Samson?), Samuel I (Do you remember the famous Seer and King Saul?), Samuel II (You surely remember the stories about King David), Kings I (The story of King Solomon and the divided kingdom), and Kings II (Tells how Israel and Judah were finally destroyed by Assyria and Babylonia). The next three books called, Isaiah, Jeremiah, and Ezekiel, give the prophecies of these men. The last twelve books are the works of other prophets, with some of whom you are not yet acquainted. They are: Hosea, Joel, Amos, Obadiah, Jonah, Micah, Nahum, Habbakuk, Zephaniah, Haggai, Zechariah, Malachi. These prophetical books were all small; so the scribes wrote them on one scroll, and called the collection the "Twelve."

The third and last division of the Bible, named Ketubim (Holy Writings), is made up of thirteen books. Many of them are very famous. They are: Psalms, Proverbs, Job, Song of Songs, Ruth, Lamentations, Ecclesiastes, Esther, Daniel, Ezra, Nehemiah, Chronicles I and Chronicles II.

Thus we learn that our Bible is made up of thirty-nine books which are divided into three sections, Torah, Nebiim, and Ketubim.

Many Jews believe that the Torah (the five books of Moses) is so wonderful that no man could have written it. They say that God Himself gave the Torah to Moses, who passed it on to Joshua. From him the

Five Books were handed down from generation to generation until they came into the hands of the Anshe Keneset Ha-gedolah who had them copied and distributed among the people. Most people also realize that the other two sections—the Nebiim and the Ketubim—are likewise holy and deserve careful study.

Besides arranging and copying those books of the Bible, which were known at that time, the Anshe Keneset Ha-gedolah made sure that the people learned their contents. Following the example of Ezra, they had the Torah read to the people in the market place, in the Temple, and in the synagogues built for those who lived too far from the Temple. Outside of Palestine, too, the Jews began a regular study of their holy books. They read them whenever they assembled in their synagogues. Thus the books became widely known, and their laws were accepted as the guide to the Jewish way of life not only in Palestine but in other lands as well.

While the Bible was not completed by the Anshe Keneset Ha-gedolah, its beginning was the first great achievement since the Jews had rebuilt the Temple. We still study this Book and try to live in accordance with the ideas of the men who wrote it. During the coming years you will have the opportunity to study the Bible in detail.

Answer carefully, the questions given in Topic IV.

V. WHY DO WE CELEBRATE PURIM?

One of the books in the section Ketubim is of particular interest to us now because it tells why we celebrate

Purim, a holiday which came into being at that time. The story, as told in the Book of Esther, is very exciting. It will be repeated here, briefly.

About 2300 years ago, some two hundred years after Cyrus allowed the Jews to return to Palestine, a foolish king, called Ahasuerus, ruled Persia. One day a counsellor of his, Haman, was angered by a Jew, named Mordecai. In his wrath, Haman decided to destroy the Jew and all his people as well. The counsellor came to Ahasuerus and told him that the Jews were not good citizens, paid no attention to his laws, and refused to pay their taxes. The king believed Haman and gave him permission to wipe out the Jewish people. At once, Haman informed the Persians that on the 13th day of the Jewish month Adar, they should attack and kill all the Jews living in Persia.

Fortunately, Mordecai found out about this order, and told his cousin Esther, who was Ahasuerus' queen, what Haman was planning to do. At the risk of her life, Esther came before the king and begged him to save her and her fellow-Jews from the hands of Haman and his followers. The King was moved with pity for Esther and her people. He realized that Haman's charges were untrue and was sorry that he had ever believed his lies. He ordered that Haman be hanged, and permitted the Jews to collect arms and defend themselves against their enemies. No one then dared to hurt the Jews, and so they were saved. The 14th of Adar thus became a day of rejoicing.

At the risk of her life, Esther came before the king and begged him to save her and her fellow-Jews.

To this day, we celebrate Purim on that date. It is a merry festival. On the eve of Purim, we read the Megillah (scroll) in which the story of Esther is told. Every time Haman is mentioned, children sound their noisemakers. During the day gifts are exchanged among family and friends. In the evening a Seudah (banquet) is held to mark the close of the festival in a jolly spirit.

There are other books in the Bible that are almost as interesting. Think of the stories of Joseph, Moses, Joshua, and the judges. But even those books which do not have exciting stories are fascinating when you understand and appreciate them. Surely they are well worth studying.

The Bible was popular among the Jews from the very time it was prepared. Men and women came frequently to the synagogues to read and learn it. The Anshe Keneset Ha-gedolah wanted also to help the people pray to God and made up several prayers for them. Thus began the Siddur (prayerbook) which we still use. The Tefillah (prayer) so called because it best expresses the Jewish faith in God and calls upon Him to protect us, as He did our fathers in ancient days, is one of the prayers written at that time.

The years during which Palestine belonged to Persia were, after all, fruitful years. The Jews rebuilt their Temple, learned to understand their religious laws, and, thanks to the Anshe Keneset Ha-gedolah, made up at least in part, the Bible and the Siddur.

Answer the questions to Topic V.

ADDITIONAL READING

The Prayerbook. Your Siddur has some interesting things to tell about the Anshe Keneset Ha-gedolah.

If you have the *Union Prayerbook* turn to p. 150 and read the first paragraph. Remember that the "Great Assembly" is the same as Anshe Keneset Ha-gedolah. "Deliberate" means "careful"; "disciples" means "students"; "a fence around the Torah" means a series of laws which will make it hard for any one to disobey the laws in the Torah.

If you have the *Authorized Daily Prayer Book* read page 184, Chapter 1, verse 1.

While you are holding the Siddur, you may want to read the Tefillah prepared by the Great Assembly.

In the *Union Prayerbook,* pages 14 and 16.

In the *Authorized Daily Prayer Book,* pages 44 ff.

The Bible. The order of the books is given in the Bible (Jewish Publication Society) on page xvi.

The Book of Esther explaining Purim is found on pages 997–1006. Chap. 3, page 999, is most interesting.

The Unconquered. The story of Purim is beautifully told in "The Messenger from Shushan," page 30.

SOMETHING TO THINK ABOUT

1. Haman, Mordecai, and Esther must have lived about 2300 years ago. Why should we celebrate Purim *this* year?
2. Were the Anshe Keneset Ha-gedolah right in hiding those books which they did not consider holy?

What Divided the Jews into Parties?

FOR many years the Jews lived happily in Palestine. With the help of the Anshe Keneset Hagedolah, they learned the Torah and lived according to its laws. At the same time, homes were rebuilt and furnished, streets were improved, and cities grew larger and more attractive. Every Jew worked earnestly to make Palestine a happy homeland for the Jewish people.

Not only were the Jews at peace with one another, but with the world outside as well. The Persian rulers allowed the Jews to live as they wished so long as they paid the necessary taxes to their treasurers and sent men to the army.

I. HOW PALESTINE BECAME PART OF THE GREAT EMPIRE

This situation was changed however, after the Greeks conquered the Persians, about 200 years after Cyrus had permitted the Jews to return to Palestine. The difference was not great at first.

The conqueror, King Alexander, did nothing to harm the Jews. On the contrary, Alexander is said to have visited the Temple in Jerusalem and to have brought a sacrifice to God to show that he was a friend of the Jews.

There is an interesting story told in connection with King Alexander's visit to Jerusalem. Shortly after the Persian armies had fallen before the mighty Greek hosts, the Kohen Gadol received a message from King Alexander saying that Palestine must become a part of the Greek Empire. The Kohen had heard that the Greeks had conquered the Persians and knew that the Jews were not strong enough to stop the Greeks. Yet he felt that it would be wrong for Him to allow the Greeks to make Palestine part of their Empire, for he had sworn to be faithful to the Persian King. The Kohen Gadol, therefore, told the messenger that he could not surrender Palestine to him.

Then the Kohen Gadol learned that Alexander himself was coming to Jerusalem at the head of a large army. Fearing that the Jews would be attacked, the Kohen Gadol decided to meet Alexander before he reached Jerusalem and tell him that he, the Jewish leader, was ready to do what the king of the Greeks demanded. Accompanied by the Kohanim and Levites of the Temple, all dressed in their white Temple robes, the Kohen Gadol went to meet Alexander. What was his surprise when he saw the king dismount from his horse and bow before him! One of Alexander's officers asked him why he bowed before the Jew. Alexander replied that the Kohen Gadol had come to him in a dream and showed him how to win an important battle. For this reason, Alexander was sure that the Kohen Gadol served a great God and deserved special respect. So Alexander treated the Jews kindly.

In your Workbook answer the questions to Topic I of Chapter 6.

II. HOW DID THE GREEK RULE DIFFER FROM THE PERSIAN?

For many years, it seemed that the change in rulers was going to make no change in the lives of the Jews. They simply paid taxes to a Greek instead of a Persian governor. The taxes were not increased. The Greek governor did not change any laws in Palestine and allowed the Jews to keep their own judges. Indeed, the Jews were given special privileges. A biblical law required that they should work on their farms and vineyards only six years out of seven. Whenever this "Seventh Year" occurred, the taxes were not collected. Also, men who joined the Greek army were allowed to rest on the Sabbath day and to observe the other laws of their religion as well. And so the Jews continued to live according to the Torah. The Kohen Gadol and his advisors, the Anshe Keneset Hagedolah, ruled over them just as they had done when Palestine belonged to Persia.

Unfortunately, King Alexander died a few years later, and then trouble began for the Jews. Several generals who had fought under Alexander wanted to take his place and rule over the lands which he had conquered. Naturally, war broke out among them. They fought in Palestine as well as in other

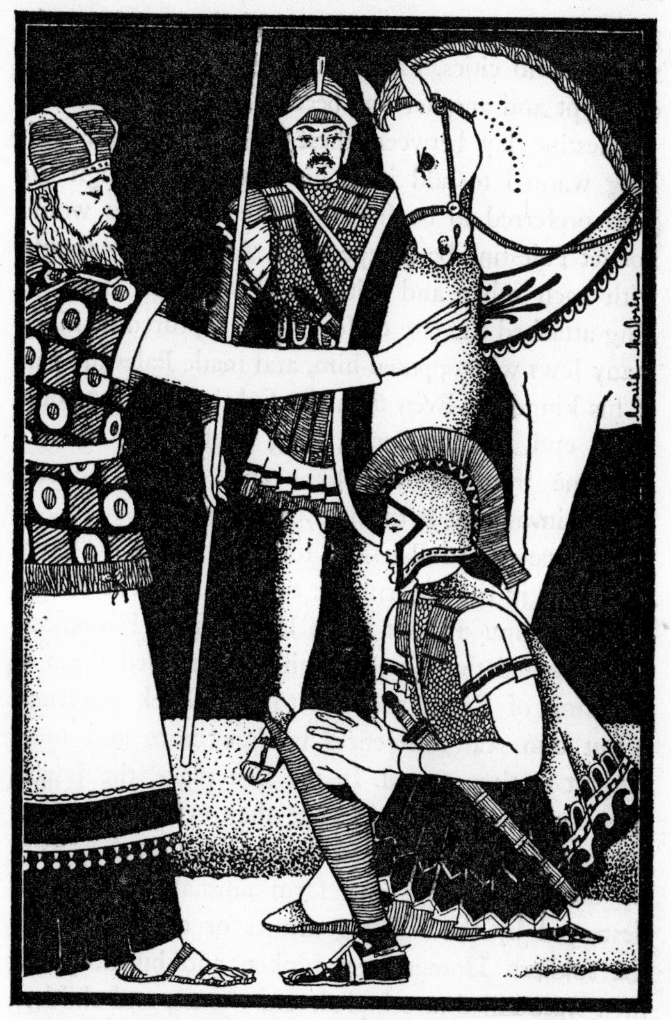

What was his surprise when he saw the king dismount from his horse and bow before him!

parts of the world and destroyed farms, vineyards, villages, and cities. Finally, one general became king of Egypt and another one became king of Syria.

Palestine lay between these two lands; and each king wanted to add it to his kingdom, though the Jews preferred to be free. But the two kings would not let Palestine be independent. And so they fought with each other and with the Jews. The Egyptian king attacked the city of Jerusalem, captured it, killed many Jews who opposed him, and made Palestine part of his kingdom. Even then the fighting did not come to an end, for the Syrian king kept trying to take Palestine from the Egyptians and, finally, he succeeded in adding it to his own kingdom.

The transfer of Palestine to Egypt made no great difference in the government of the Jews. The Kohen Gadol continued to act as the Jewish ruler. His officers still collected the taxes though they handed them to the king of Egypt and not to the Greek governor.

But two real differences became more and more evident as time passed. In the first place, the Jewish farmers were becoming poorer than ever before. War always brings poverty, and the wars fought then were no exception. Crops and farm animals were either destroyed by the fighting armies or taken away by the soldiers. Homes were broken and burnt, young men were killed or crippled, and women and children were often left to starve. No wonder the Jews of Palestine hated war and all who made war. Many years had passed before the farmers were again able to support themselves. Some never succeeded, and were forced to depend on charity. These people found comfort only in their religion and they began to study the Bible and to obey the laws contained in it more carefully than ever before. They thus became Hasidim (Pious men).

Answer the questions to Topic II.

III. WHY DID JEWS BECOME HELLENISTS?

A second difference in the life of the Jews first became noticeable among the richer Jews, the merchants, and the wealthy land owners. These Jews had learned from the Greek merchants how to manage important business undertakings and were thus able to increase their wealth. These Jews, therefore, admired the Greeks. Besides, the Greeks dressed in fine clothes and lived in beautiful houses, decorated with artistic pictures and statues. Very often they celebrated festivals at which men and women danced to the music of Greek instruments, and drank much wine. They went to the theatre to see interesting plays and to hear beautiful music. What the Greeks enjoyed most were athletic contests. Once in four years they used to arrange Olympic games in honor of their chief god, Zeus. On those occasions people came from far and near to the large field in Athens, the most important Greek city, in order to watch the contests. And they were very exciting.

Before the festivities began, a sacrifice was brought to the idol, Zeus. Then beautiful poems and stories of Greek life were recited. And then came the show. When the foot-races were announced, over a hundred athletes lined up. These runners were the best in the world. They had been trained in the gymnasiums of their home cities. So that the people might distinguish them from one another, each wore a hat or carried a shield with some special design on it. The winner of the race was crowned with a wreath of olive branches. His name was announced and he became as popular a hero among the Greeks as Babe Ruth or Jack Dempsey now are among the Americans.

The other contests were equally interesting. There were wrestling matches, spear-throwing contests, and, most exciting of all, chariot races. The winner of each contest was crowned with a wreath and cheered to the skies. The Olympic games were new to the people living in or near Palestine, and they were eager to see them. Many Jews, in their eagerness to see the exciting contests, were even willing to look on while sacrifices were being offered to Zeus.

The Greeks were admired for an additional reason. Among them were some wise men who wrote interesting books; and the Jews also enjoyed reading these books.

The rich Jews had means with which to pay for entertainment, and had leisure for pleasurable activities. And so they began to imitate the Greeks. They wore Greek clothes, learned to read Greek books, decorated their homes like the Greeks, and even attended drinking parties. Thus as the rich Jews became more and more Greek, they grew less and less Jewish.

Answer the questions to Topic III.

IV. WHY DID SOME JEWS BECOME HASIDIM?

At first, no one paid much attention to what the rich Jews did because there were so few of them. But now more Jews were becoming wealthy. An ever-increasing number were learning from the Greeks how to be successful merchants. Then, too, the Jew who was appointed by the Egyptian king to collect taxes from all the peoples living in and near Palestine employed many Jews as his assistants. Since they were allowed to keep a certain portion of the taxes, they too became rich. As the number of rich Jews increased, so did the number of Hellenists (people who lived like the Greeks). In a hunderd years, a large proportion of the Jewish people had become Hellenized.

These Hellenists wanted to build a gymnasium in Jerusalem, where they might train themselves to become athletes, so that they might participate in the Olympic games. They wanted to decorate the houses and streets of the city with Greek statues and buildings. In fact, they would have liked to make Jerusalem look like a Greek city, and the people in it like Greeks. However, the Kohen Gadol refused to permit any one to build a gymnasium or to set up Greek statues in the city; and he had good reasons for his action.

In the first place, the Hellenists in attending the Olympic Games were indirectly honoring the idol,

There were wrestling matches, spear-throwing contests, and most exciting of all, chariot races.

Zeus. Secondly, they admired athletes more than religious leaders like the prophets and Kohanim, and spent more time in the gymnasium than in the house of study. Thirdly, Hellenist writers taught the people that it was important to be clever and well-read but they did not teach them to know God nor to live in accordance with His commandments. Finally the Hellenists came to believe that beauty was more important than goodness. Such ideas, of course, were extremely hateful to *all* pious Jews as well as to the Kohen Gadol.

To make sure that they would not turn Hellenists, the pious Jews became more and more observant of their religion. They followed every law of the Bible no matter how difficult it was to obey. They spent more time than ever before in studying the Torah, for they felt that studying it would help them remain Jewish while so many others were becoming Hellenized. Thus many more Jews became Hasidim.

Answer the questions to Topic IV.

V. HOW DID HELLENISTS GET ALONG WITH HASIDIM?

The Hellenists naturally disliked the Hasidim for not letting them build a gymnasium nor decorate the streets of Jerusalem.

Often Hellenists and Hasidim met in the streets of Jerusalem. The Hasid would call the Hellenist a traitor, and in return, he would be called an old fogey. Sometimes they fought, not merely with their brains and tongues, but with their fists. Thus the conquest of Palestine by Greece led many Jews to hate and despise each other.

Most Jews were neither Hellenists nor Hasidim. They were satisfied to study Torah and live in accordance with its laws, but they also wanted to learn some of the valuable lessons which the Greeks could teach them. For instance, they learned Greek, read some good Greek books, and learned how to trade with people who lived outside of Palestine. However, they did not go to athletic contests held in honor of Greek idols. They were Jews and wanted to continue living as Jews, and not to become Greeks.

What happened to the Jews who lived outside of Palestine? Most of them could not long remain Hasidim, but neither did they become completely Hellenized. They found speaking Hebrew in a foreign land very difficult and many of them forgot it. However, they were still anxious to know the Torah, and obey its laws. Indeed, they were so proud of their "book" that they wanted their Greek neighbors to know what was in it. And so it happened that at this time the Bible was, for the first time, translated into a foreign language, Greek. Since that time the Bible has been translated into so many different languages that it may be read in almost any language that is spoken.

How the Kohen Gadol felt about the Hellenists, you can guess from the fact that he did not let them build a gymnasium or decorate the streets with Greek statues. A great number of the Kohanim, however, were secretly Hellenistic, but did not dare to let anyone know it. Later on they showed themselves in their true colors.

Their opportunity came when Palestine again changed masters. The king of Syria finally succeeded in driving the Egyptian army out of Palestine and adding this bit of land to his own large kingdom, Syria. At first, the Syrian king did nothing to help the Hellenists. But some years after his death a new ruler arose over Syria, a king who was cruel and ambitious, a king who wanted to conquer the whole world. Then —but that is the story of our next chapter.

Answer the questions to Topic V.

ADDITIONAL READING

The Unconquered. How Alexander became master of Palestine is told in "Alexander Meets Simon" beginning on page 71.

How the Bible was first translated into Greek is told in "Seventy-Two Scribes." The story begins on page 83.

How a Jew was appointed to a high office by an Egyptian king is told in "A Boy Ambassador," beginning on page 92.

The Great March. Read "With Peace They Conquer" pages 10–17.

SOMETHING TO THINK ABOUT

1. Suppose you lived 2200 years ago. Would you have joined the Hellenists or the Hasidim? Why?

Why Was Hanukkah First Celebrated?

THE coming of the Greeks to Palestine caused serious differences among the Jews. Those who liked the Greek festivals, games, ornaments, clothes, language, and books became known as Hellenists. Those who preferred to study the Torah and live according to their ancient customs and laws took the name of Hasidim. These two groups disliked each other. Hellenists considered the Hasidim old-fashioned and despised them. Hasidim thought the Hellenists were traitors to the Jewish religion and hated them.

For a long time—for over a hundred years, in fact—the two groups of Jews lived side by side. They often quarrelled but never really harmed each other. During that time a king of Syria took Palestine away from Egypt and made it part of his own kingdom, without making any important changes in the life of the people.

I. HOW A HELLENIST BECAME KOHEN GADOL

But 2100 years ago—150 years after Alexander had conquered the Persians and made Palestine part of the Greek empire—a Syrian ruler took advantage of the

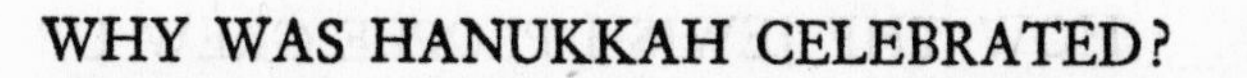

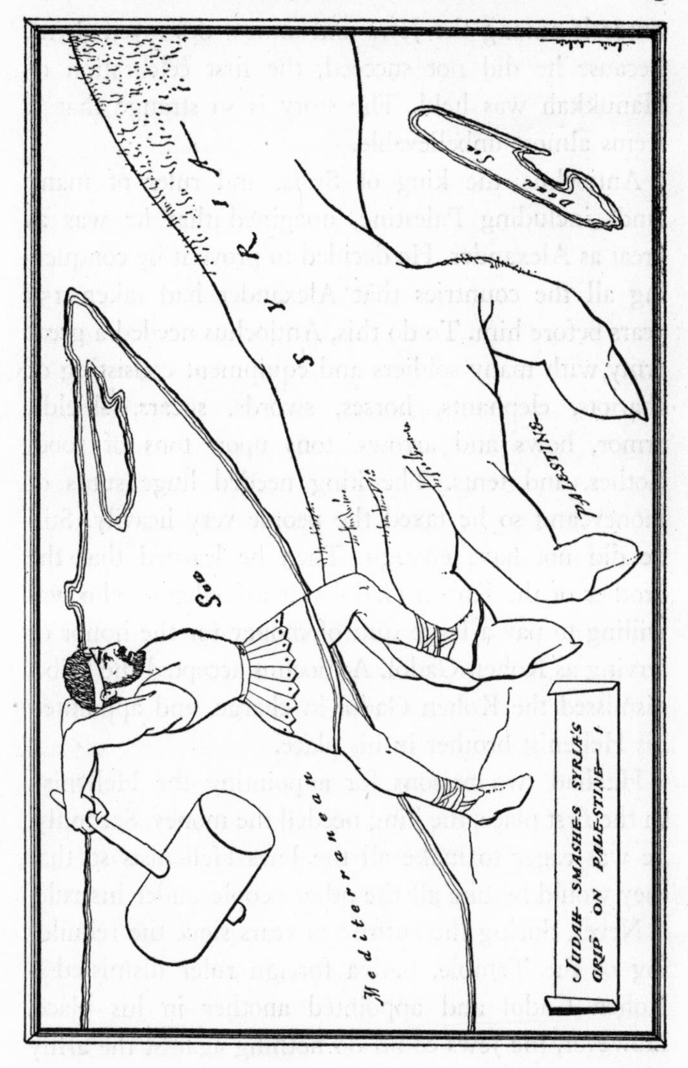
Judah smashes Syria's grip on Palestine—!
Mediterranean
Sea
S Y R I A
Dead S
PALESTINE

quarrels among the Jews and almost destroyed them. Because he did not succeed, the first celebration of Hanukkah was held. The story is so strange that it seems almost unbelievable.

Antiochus, the king of Syria, and ruler of many lands including Palestine, imagined that he was as great as Alexander. He decided to prove it by conquering all the countries that Alexander had taken 150 years before him. To do this, Antiochus needed a great army with many soldiers and equipment consisting of chariots, elephants, horses, swords, spears, shields, armor, bows and arrows, tons upon tons of food, clothes, and tents. The king needed huge sums of money and so he taxed the people very heavily. Still he did not have enough. Then he learned that the brother of the Kohen Gadol was a Hellenist who was willing to pay a large sum of money for the honor of serving as Kohen Gadol. Antiochus accepted the bribe, dismissed the Kohen Gadol in charge, and appointed his Hellenist brother in his place.

He had two reasons for appointing the Hellenist. In the first place, the king needed the money. Secondly, he was eager to make all the Jews Hellenists so that they would be like all the other people under his rule.

Never, during the entire 350 years since the rebuilding of the Temple, had a foreign ruler dismissed a Kohen Gadol and appointed another in his place. However, the Jews could do nothing against the army of Syrian soldiers whom Antiochus had sent to force the Jews to accept the new man as Kohen Gadol.

A few years later the king expelled the Kohen Gadol whom he himself had appointed, and replaced him with another one, even more completely Hellenistic. The new Kohen Gadol, Menelaus, did not even belong to the family of the Kohanim, all of whom were expected to be children of Kohanim. He received his appointment by bribing the Syrian king with a huge sum of gold. The Hasidim were now more indignant than before; but they had to obey the new Kohen Gadol because the Syrian soldiers forced them to do so. The Hellenists, on the other hand, were happy. They no longer had to follow the ancient customs for fear of punishment at the hands of the officers of the Kohen Gadol. They went to the gymnasium or theatre instead of the Temple or Synagogue, read Greek books instead of the Bible, dressed in Greek clothes and even worshipped Greek gods.

Answer the questions to Topic I of Chapter 7.

II. HOW THE PEOPLE FELT ABOUT MENELAUS

To make sure he would not be dismissed, Menelaus stole some of the treasures kept in the Temple and gave them to Antiochus. He knew that only as long as Antiochus' soldiers defended him, would he hold his high position.

When the people found out that their Kohen Gadol had taken the Temple treasures and given them to Antiochus, they lost all patience. Even the Hellenists were shocked. Excited men and women gathered in the streets of Jerusalem. With sticks and stones, they attacked the soldiers who guarded the Kohen Gadol. When Antiochus learned what had happened, he sent his soldiers to punish the people. The Syrians attacked Jerusalem on the Sabbath, when the Jews would not fight, even to save their lives. They broke through the walls of the city, killed many Jews, and robbed the Temple of its treasures. The Jews were forced to wait for another opportunity to drive the hated Menelaus out of the Temple.

One day the rumor was spread in Jerusalem that Antiochus had been killed in battle. People quickly gathered near the Temple, attacked the soldiers who were guarding Menelaus, and killed many of them. Menelaus himself was forced to hide till the danger was over.

Answer the questions to Topic II.

III. THE MAD KING'S REVENGE

But the story of the king's death had been false. Word of what had happened in Jerusalem reached him when he was in a very bad mood. In his anger, King Antiochus decided to destroy the people that had dared to rise up against his soldiers and against the man whom he had appointed as their ruler. Once more his soldiers broke into Jerusalem, killed every Hasid they could find, and drove out all those who were not Hellenists. But Antiochus was not yet satisfied. He turned to the Hellenists for advice on how to destroy Judaism. Menelaus, though he himself was a Jew and though he was in charge of the Temple, then advised Antiochus that if he wanted the Jewish people to disappear, he should force them to give up worshipping their God and following the Commandments of the Torah.

Antiochus decided to follow the Kohen's advice. He ordered that the holy Temple be made a place of worship for the Greek idol, Zeus. Syrian soldiers then put a statue of Zeus in the Temple, brought unclean animals into the courtyard, erected an altar to their god, and brought him sacrifices. The light of the Menorah, which faithful Kohanim had kept burning during the 350 years in which the Temple had stood, was put out. In addition, Antiochus announced that Jews who were caught keeping the Sabbath, studying the Torah, or praying to God, would be put to death.

To carry out the mad king's orders, soldiers went from city to city and from town to town; they built altars to Zeus and forced the Jews to worship the idol. Wherever they found a copy of the Torah, they destroyed it. Those who refused to give up their religion were cruelly murdered.

There are many stories of heroes who died rather than obey the orders of Antiochus. An old man, Eliezer, refused to taste the flesh of a swine. The soldiers beat him to death. Hannah and her seven sons would not bow down to an idol; the children were tortured to death and the mother, herself, was killed. Over a thousand Jews, caught observing the Sabbath in a cave, were murdered. Not one of those men raised a hand to defend himself, because it was a Jewish custom not to fight on the Sabbath.

Desperately, the people tried to escape the soldiers of Antiochus. Many fled from their homes and hid in caves. Others made believe that they were Greek, but secretly obeyed the laws of the Torah. Yet large numbers suffered death, and the rest lived in constant fear of being captured. It soon became clear to those Hasidim who were still alive that without a leader to help them, the Jewish people would be destroyed.

Answer the questions to Topic III.

IV. THE BEGINNING OF THE REVOLT

Judah Maccabee then appeared. He became known when he, together with his father Mattathias, and his four brothers, came to the market place of their city, Modin, at the command of Syrian officers. There an altar to Zeus had been set up. Immediately Judah knew what was about to happen. He knew also what his father would do and he prepared for trouble. A soldier brought a swine which was to be sacrificed to Zeus. The officer in charge then addressed Judah's father, Mattathias, the leading Jew in Modin.

"O, Mattathias, thou art a ruler and an honorable and great man in this city. Come thou first and do the commandment of the king."

Judah held his breath. What would his father answer? He had not long to wait. Mattathias answered in a loud voice:

"If all the nations hearken unto him, yet will I and my sons and my brethren walk in the covenant of the fathers!"

Judah thrilled. It was wonderful to have a father like that. But what was this? A Hellenist was coming forward to bring the unclean sacrifice. Judah looked at his father's face and knew at once that the moment for action had arrived. With dagger in hand, the old man sprang forward and struck the traitor to the earth. When the officer leaped at Mattathias, Judah and his brothers ran to his aid. But the old man was ahead of them. He killed the Syrian and shouted: "Whoever is for the Lord, follow me!" Mattathias, with Judah and his other sons at his side, then fell upon the soldiers. The men of Modin came to their aid. It was not long before the handful of soldiers who were still alive, fled from the town.

Mattathias knew well that more soldiers would soon come to Modin to punish him and his sons. He, therefore, fled to a cave in the mountains. To him came all the Hasidim who preferred to die rather than to disobey the laws of the Torah and of God. Many of these had read a book called "Daniel" which had been written at that time. It is now a part of our Bible. The book told how certain Jews had suffered, just because they had obeyed the laws of God. But in the end, the wicked ones had been punished and the Jews had been saved. The book prophesied that Syria, too, would be destroyed because its king was so cruel and unjust.

The Book of Daniel gave the men courage to fight against the strong Syrian armies. The little band attacked and destroyed many troops of Syrian soldiers who had been sent to look for them. They took the

Judah . . . ordered his soldiers to clean up the Temple.

armor and weapons of the Syrians and returned to their hiding place, to lie in wait for more soldiers.

When Mattathias died, his brave son, Judah Maccabee, took his place as leader. Many more men came to join his army. Some of them were not Hasidim. They had, in fact, been admirers of the Hellenists, who had learned their error when they saw how cruelly Antiochus had treated the Jewish people. These men came to help save their people from destruction.

Answer the questions to Topic IV.

V. THE HAPPY ENDING

Now Judah was a bold and determined fighter. Instead of hiding as his father had, in a cave, he went fearlessly to meet the enemy. With a small army of less than 3,000 men, he fought and defeated a Syrian army many times larger than his. A second army was sent against him and a third, but Judah was victorious every time.

One of these battles, Judah won by a clever trick. He learned that half of the Syrian army, which in itself was many times bigger than his whole army, was planning to attack him at night. He left the campfires burning to make the enemy believe he was still in camp, and, stealing his way up a mountain road, surprised the other half. Judah attacked and easily defeated it. He seized many arms and a great deal of money which he used for his own soldiers. When the other half of the Syrian army returned to its camp, tired out with its useless chase, Judah fell upon these soldiers and defeated them, too. The only Syrians who were left alive and free were those who fled.

After two years of hard fighting, Judah finally captured the city of Jerusalem and drove out the Hellenist Kohen Gadol, Menelaus, who had been helping the Syrians. Judah then ordered his soldiers to clean up the Temple. The statue of Zeus was thrown out, the altar on which unclean animals had been sacrificed, was destroyed. The damaged parts of the Temple were repaired and the golden vessels stolen by the Syrians, were replaced.

On the 25th day of Kislev, which usually falls in December, the Temple was once more ready for use. The Jews celebrated its rededication (setting aside for holy use), and the ceremony became known by its Hebrew name, Hanukkah, which means "dedication." Judah took the place of the Kohen Gadol and made a thank-offering to God for His help. Beginning with the 25th day of Kislev, the Jews feasted for eight days, in honor of the rededication. At Judah's suggestion, these days were set aside to be celebrated as a holiday for ever after. For this reason, we are still celebrating Hanukkah to this day.

On the eve of the 25th day of Kislev, we light a little candle to remind us of those great days when Judah Maccabee rededicated the Temple. Every night thereafter we light one candle more than the night before. On the last evening of Hanukkah, eight little candles are burning brightly, casting their cheery light over the entire house.

A legend tells how we happen to be lighting candles on Hanukkah. At the time of the dedication (Hanukkah), the Kohanim looked about for oil with which to re-light the Menorah, whose light had been put out by the Syrians. They found only one small container of oil. It looked as if it might be enough for one day. But to their great joy, that small amount of oil lasted for eight days. By that time, fresh oil had been secured by the Kohanim, and the Menorah could be kept burning steadily.

The capture of Jerusalem and the re-dedication of the Temple did not end the war. Twenty-five years passed before the Jews finally won their freedom. Often it seemed as though the struggle would be in vain. At one time the Syrian general almost succeeded in capturing Judah and his whole army. Fortunately, the Syrians had to return home to put down a revolt against their own king. At another time, a very large Syrian army succeeded in driving Judah back. In that battle his brother, Eliezer, lost his life when he killed a huge elephant on which he thought the king of Syria was riding. The huge animal fell upon Eliezer and crushed him. Shortly after that battle, Judah Maccabee himself was killed. There was great sorrow among the Jews. They feared that the hard fighting and the victories which Judah had won would be in vain.

But Jonathan, clever and brave brother of Judah, carried on the fight. A third brother was killed in battle but Jonathan continued. Meanwhile, more re-

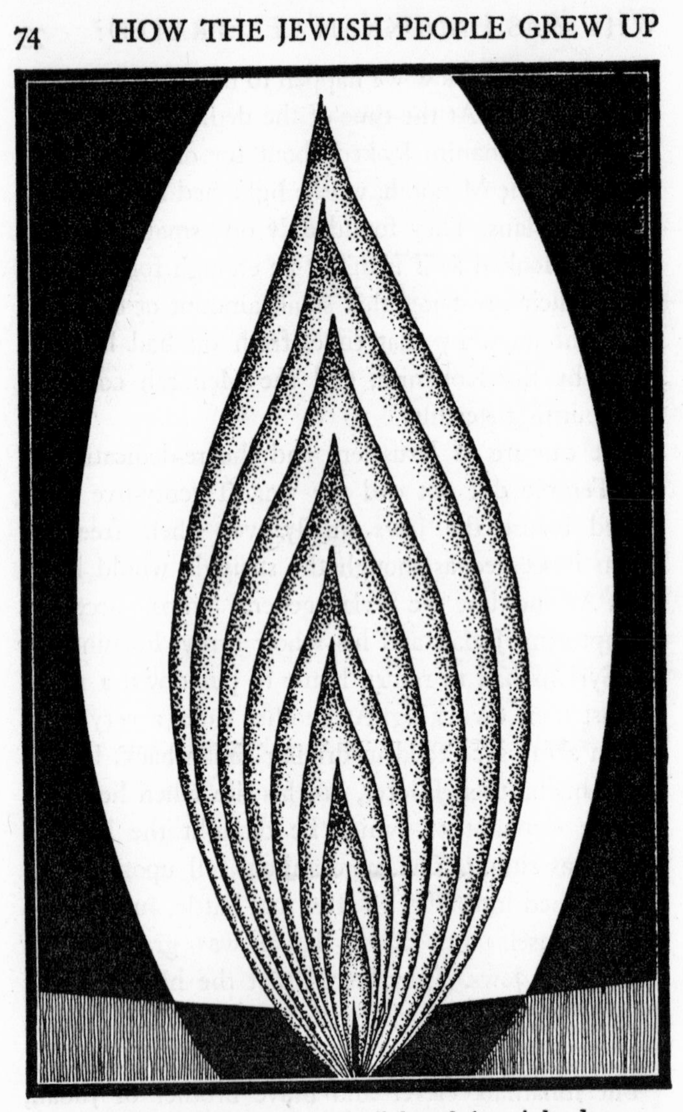

. . . that small amount of oil lasted for eight days.

volts were taking place in Syria. The king had to defend himself and could not carry on an additional war. He, therefore, became a friend of Jonathan and appointed him Kohen Gadol.

The harsh laws of King Antiochus were withdrawn. The Hellenists lost their power. The revolt against Syria seemed to be successful.

And then a Syrian general treacherously murdered Jonathan. The fifth brother, Simon, now became leader and Kohen Gadol in place of Jonathan and carried on the fight for freedom. The Syrian king, tired of trying to conquer the Jews, granted them complete freedom. For the first time in the 400 years that had passed since Babylonia first conquered Judea, Palestine had no foreign rulers.

Answer the questions to Topic V.

ADDITIONAL READING

Prayerbook. In the *Union Prayerbook* we have a summary of the Hanukkah story taken from the Book of Maccabees which is in the Apocrypha (not the Bible). It is found on pages 49–51.

In the *Authorized Daily Prayer Book* we have a special prayer at the top of page 52.

Apocrypha. If you are ambitious, read parts of the Book of Maccabees. It is found on pages 210–258 in the Edition of the *Apocrypha* according to the Authorized Version issued by the Oxford Press.

The law of Antiochus declaring Jews must become like others is given on page 212, Chap. 1, verses 41–50.

Mattathias and the King's officers: pages 213-214, Chapter 2, verses 15-28.

How Jews died rather than fight on the Sabbath—page 214, Chapter 2, verses 32-38.

How Hanukkah was celebrated for the first time—page 221, Chapter 4, verses 52-59.

Bible. The Book of Daniel, you recall, gave the Hasidim courage to fight. It is found in your Bible, pages 1007-1026. The book contains two famous stories. The first tells of those Jews who were cast into a burning furnace but came out alive. Read page 1011, Chapter 3, verses 13-26. Read page 1017, Chapter 6, verses 17-24.

The Unconquered. The stories in this book are so enjoyable that it is not necessary to tell you anything more about them. If you have time, read: "The Fiery Steed," beginning on page 115; "Seven Sacrifices" page 135; "Judas the Maccabee," page 148; "A Knave's End," p. 157.

The Great March. Here are two other stories worth reading. "Follow Me"—pages 18-21; "Fight for Right" pages 22-29.

SOMETHING TO THINK ABOUT

1. Hanukkah is celebrated in honor of the rededication of the Altar in the Temple. We do not celebrate the great victories of the Maccabees. Why?
2. Why did Antiochus believe that a loyal Jew could not be a loyal Syrian?

How Did the Jews Live during Their Independence?

FREE! Free at last! Hurrah, for the Maccabees!

These cries sounded from one end of Palestine to the other, when the joyful news spread that Palestine had become an independent country. There was good reason for rejoicing. No longer would the Jews of Palestine have to obey the laws of foreign rulers. The commandments of God, as written in the Torah, would now be the only laws to follow. Their hard-earned money would no longer be paid out in taxes to foreign lands. It would be used for increasing their own comfort in their own land. And best of all, their young men need no longer serve in the armies of Persia, Greece, Egypt, or Syria. They could remain peacefully in their own homes.

1. HOW WERE THE JEWS GOVERNED?

The Jews did not forget the Maccabees. Simon, the only one of the five brothers still alive, was made Kohen Gadol and Prince of the Jews. When, some years later, he, too, fell by the hand of a murderer, his brave son Yohanan became the ruler. From that time on, until Palestine again lost its independence, only

The Commandments of God, as written in the Torah, would now be the only laws to follow.

the descendants of this family were appointed kings.

How did the Jews fare during their independence? A study of the Jewish government in the days of the Hasmoneans—as the family of the Maccabees was known—helps us understand the life of the people. The leader was, of course, the Hasmonean ruler. He was both king and Kohen Gadol. He was head of the army; he appointed the important officers, decided when it was necessary to go to war, and how much the people should pay in taxes. He was also in charge of the Temple, and conducted the services.

But the Hasmonean ruler could not do everything simply because it pleased him. The people had a written set of laws—the Torah—and the king had to obey its commandments just as fully as any other Jew. He had also a council composed of the leading men in Judea who advised him on all important matters. This body of men was called the Sanhedrin. The members met regularly in the Temple and discussed everything important that concerned the country. Their president, the Kohen Gadol, and king had to abide by their decisions.

Besides acting as advisory council to the Hasmoneans, the Sanhedrin served also as the highest court of the land. It settled disputes that were too difficult for the judges of the ordinary city courts, and tried men who committed very serious crimes for which they might be put to death.

The Sanhedrin's greatest task was to make the people live according to the law, contained mostly in the Torah which was known as the Written Law. But there were a great many laws and customs which had grown up among the Jews and were not written down in the Torah. Thus, the celebration of Hanukkah is not mentioned in the Bible, yet it was and still is faithfully observed among Jews. No commandment of the Bible directs the Jews to pray regularly, yet it was well understood that Jews should do so. The Bible commands us to study the Torah, but it does not require us to read a certain portion each Sabbath morning. Jewish custom, however, demands that we read a definite section called "Sidra" on each Sabbath morning. There are a great many other laws and customs which are not written in the Torah, but are, nevertheless, observed by the Jews. Such laws and customs are known as the "Oral Law."

Answer the questions to Topic I of Chapter 8.

II. WHAT WERE THE DIFFERENCES BETWEEN THE SADDUCEES AND PHARISEES?

The existence of the Oral Law brought the Sanhedrin face to face with a number of difficult problems. Should they or should they not expect all Jews to observe the Oral Law? Should they punish any one who failed to observe the Oral Law? How? As you might expect, the members of the Sanhedrin did not all agree.

The learned Soferim realized that the Torah itself could not possibly give all the laws in detail, and was as a result not clear enough to guide the people. The Sanhedrin was obliged to draw up a clear set of directions for the guidance of the people. Thus the Torah says: "An eye for an eye." But the Soferim had too much respect for the Torah to believe that it actually meant that if one put out another's eye, he was to lose his own eye. Such punishment was cruel and did not help the one who had lost his eye. They, therefore, insisted that such a law must be explained to mean that one must pay with money or goods if he has hurt another in any way. Sometimes a question arose to which the Bible seemed to have no answer. The Soferim, however, felt certain that the Torah came from God and therefore contained solutions of all important problems. These solutions could be found if the Torah were studied diligently. And to be sure, an answer would be found! The answer did not, perhaps, seem very clear at first. But the Soferim made it clear by giving it the meaning which, to them, seemed most sensible. As all these explanations were considered part of the Oral Law, the Soferim felt that it was important for every Jew to know and obey it as carefully as the Written Law.

But the high officers, the leading Kohanim, and the rich landowners, did not agree with the learned men. Explanations of the Torah, they felt were unnecessary. If no clear answer to a question could be found in the Bible, then they were prepared to make up their own answers. Moreover, if any law in the Bible seemed cruel or harsh, these men felt it should still be obeyed, because it was part of the Written Law, which every Jew was bound to obey. They, therefore, felt that the

Oral Law was unnecessary and need not be observed. As most of them belonged to the leading families of the Kohanim, they called themselves Zaddukim after Zadok who had been Kohen Gadol in the days of Solomon. In English, we call them Sadducees.

The Sadducees had no respect for those who disagreed with them. Since they were the leaders, they considered the others as "Perushim" (a Hebrew word meaning those who separated themselves from the rest of the people). In English we call them Pharisees.

Pharisees and Sadducees did not get along well with each other. The Pharisees were interested mostly in making the people more religious and more learned in the law. The Sadducees tried to make Palestine a richer and more powerful country; they wanted it to be strong enough to conquer the small nations round about and to withstand the possible attack of a mighty nation.

Each party tried to induce the king to choose the majority of the Sanhedrin from among its followers. Usually, the king chose a majority of Sadducees because he was himself a Sadducee. But he also selected several leading Pharisees for the Sanhedrin. He had three reasons for doing so.

1. Most of the Jews respected the Pharisees rather than the Sadducees. If there were no Pharisee members in the Sanhedrin, the people might refuse to obey its laws.

2. The Sanhedrin was the highest court in the land. Some of its members had to be very learned in the

Torah, in order to conduct trials and reach decisions in accordance with the law. Only the Pharisees were sufficiently learned.

3. Some laws of the Torah were not clearly understood by the people, and it was the duty of the Sanhedrin to explain them. The Pharisees were the only men capable of doing this.

Answer the questions to Topic II.

III. HOW DID THE SADDUCEES HELP THEIR PEOPLE?

For many years Sadducees and Pharisees worked, each group in its own way, to improve the life of the people. The Sadducees were largely responsible for the increased wealth that came to Palestine, by making trading easy and profitable. Before that time, the people in Palestine used the money of other nations, and only a few people knew the value of each coin. This made it difficult for people to buy or sell. At the same time trading with foreign lands meant taking great risks. The roads were filled with robbers and a merchant was never sure that the goods he sent off would ever arrive. As for trading by sea, it was altogether impossible, because Judea had no seaport.

But the Hasmoneans, following the advice of the Sadducees overcame all these difficulties. They made coins of gold, silver, and copper, of which all the people knew the value. They set soldiers to watch the roads and thus made travel on land safe. People could now use the knowledge of business taught them by the Greeks. They traded with the countries north and east of Palestine. Camels and donkeys carrying heavy packs on their backs filled the highways and enriched their owners.

The Hasmoneans also secured a port for their people. They conquered the city of Jaffa which lies on the coast of the Mediterranean Sea and added it to their country. The business men now built ships and used them for carrying grain, fruit, wine, oils, and spices to lands where they were badly wanted and where people were ready to pay high prices for them. On their return, these ships brought back good cloth, rubber, and fine parchment—just the articles which the people in Palestine needed most.

The largest amount of business, naturally, was carried on among the Palestinian Jews themselves. Shops of all kinds were set up in the cities and the people bought and sold, very much as we do now.

For the first time in our history many Jews earned their living by engaging in business. It is interesting to note that the observance of holidays like Passover, Shabuot and Sukkot helped to improve business. On each of these festivals, Jews came to Jerusalem not only from every corner of Palestine, but from many distant lands as well. They came from Persia in the east, Syria in the north, Rome in the west, and Egypt in the south. They all met in Jerusalem to serve God and to worship in His Holy Temple. When the holidays ended, business men met the merchants from the other lands, discussed their affairs, ordered what they needed, arranged for shipping the goods and paid

Camels and donkeys carrying heavy packs on their backs filled the highways. . . .

in gold, silver, or merchandise. It was done without difficulty because they could speak to one another in Hebrew or Aramaic which all of them understood. And so the amount of trade grew and business men gained wealth.

Those not engaged in business also profited. Farmers and shepherds received higher prices than before for their grain and wool, and could live more comfortably. City laborers were kept busy building homes and shops, or manufacturing furniture, dishes, tools, and weapons. Soferim were needed to write important contracts made by business people and to copy the Books of the Bible which the Pharisees were always reading and studying. Others were employed by the king as police officers, tax-collectors, clerks, and judges. Finally, many men served in the army. There was work enough for every healthy man in those days. The sick, orphans, and widows were supported with money kept in the Temple.

The Sadducees were satisfied with their accomplishments. Did the Pharisees do as much for the Jews? Our next chapter will tell us.

Answer the questions to Topic III.

ADDITIONAL READING

Apocrypha. How Simon was murdered together with two of his sons is told in the Book of Maccabees, Chapter 16, verses 14–17.

How Yohanan (John) escaped is told in verses 21 and 22.

The Unconquered. A book now called "Ecclesiasticus" was written at the time when the Hasmoneans ruled. Its author was Jesus ben Sirach. The book is found in the Apocrypha on pages 130–190. One of its most interesting stories is given in *The Unconquered* and is called "The Fox and the Fish." You will find it on page 103.

SOMETHING TO THINK ABOUT

1. Do we Jews today live according to the ideas of the Sadducees or the Pharisees? Why do you think so?
2. Since the Hasmonean kings were usually Sadducees, why did they allow Pharisees to become members of the Sanhedrin?

How Were the Children Educated?

WHILE the Sadducees labored to strengthen the Jewish kingdom and make the people wealthier, the Pharisees tried to give the people a better understanding of Judaism and a greater knowledge of the Torah.

I. THE MAN WHO BELIEVED IN EDUCATION FOR ALL

One of their leaders, Simeon ben Shetah, an important member of the Sanhedrin, caused a law to be passed ordering the people of Jerusalem and of other cities to send their boys to school. Think of it! More than two thousand years ago, all Jewish parents were expected to send their children to school! More than two thousand years ago, our ancestors knew how important it was for everybody to go to school and study!

Even today we can still find countries where a father need not send his child to school if he does not wish to do so. It may interest you to know that many of the Arab children now living in Palestine do not attend any school. When the young Arabs grow up, most of them do not know much more than farming —and very poor farmers they are, too. They do not even know how to use modern machinery on their farms. As a result, the Palestinian Arabs are very poor. Some of them are still nomads and live as the Jews did 4000 years ago. Many cannot read or write, and they do not understand their own holy book—the Koran. How much better it would be if they could all go to a good school!

We, in America, know how necessary it is for all children to attend school. But we must remember that our Pharisee teachers, led by the wise Simeon ben Shetah, knew it 2000 years ago! And the Jews were wise enough to understand that Simeon was right. Somewhat later, they required country boys also to attend school.

There is a story told about Simeon which shows how wise the people believed him to be. Some foreign princes once came to visit the Hasmonean king who held a great feast in their honor. In the midst of the feasting one of them said: "Where is the wise man who entertained us with his learned conversation when we were here a few years ago?" The prince referred to Simeon ben Shetah! The king immediately sent for the scholar and was pleased to note how eagerly every one listened to Simeon's brilliant conversation.

Another story tells how honest Simeon was. This famous son of Shetah, was a brother of the queen, an important member of the Sanhedrin, and a well-known teacher. Yet he had to earn his living by combing flax and selling it in the market. He earned too little even to buy a donkey on which to carry the flax to market. Simeon ben Shetah was therefore compelled to carry heavy loads of flax on his shoulders. Then some of his pupils presented him with a donkey. He thanked them for the gift, but when he examined his new possession, he found, to his surprise, that a beautiful and costly diamond hung from a string about the neck of his donkey. He immediately tore the precious stone from the string, gave it to his pupils and begged them to return it to the man from whom they had bought the donkey. Simeon was very poor but much too honest to take advantage of another's mistake. Such was the character of the Pharisee teacher who first realized the need of teaching the Torah to all. We Jews may well be proud of him.

Answer the questions to Topic I of Chapter 9.

II. EDUCATION IN THE HOME

Let us now see how the teaching was done in those days. In the first place, we must realize that the school was not the only place where Jews learned their religion, history, and geography. The home, the Temple, the synagogue, and even the streets and country roads had a share in the children's education.

In the home, father and mother taught their children that there was a God in heaven, Who loved them and was ever ready to help them. They also taught them that God gave the Torah to the Jews so that they would be a holy people. Reminders of the Torah were found in every part of the house.

One bright lad noticed a piece of parchment nailed on the doorpost. When the boy asked what it was, his mother answered that it was a "mezuzah."

"What is a 'mezuzah,' mother?"

The answer was brief but clear: "A mezuzah, my child, is a piece of parchment on which an important commandment of the Torah is written. It directs parents to teach the Torah to the children."

"And what is the Torah?"

"The Torah is a set of books teaching us how to be good and loyal Jews."

"I should like to study the Torah, Mother."

"You certainly shall. Just wait till you are five years old!"

"That's a long time, mother!"

The mother smiled. Her heart was filled with joy. Soon her son, too, would study the Holy Torah.

Another time, the boy noticed his father praying. There was a little black box on his head and another one just like it on his left arm. Each was held in place by long, black, leather straps. Sonny was curious.

"Father, what are those black boxes?"

"Tefillin, my son!"

"And what are Tefillin?"

"Boxes in which portions of the Torah are kept!"

"O, yes! Mother told me that the mezuzah contains a portion of our holy Torah, too!"

"Quite right, and the most important commandment in both the mezuzah and the tefillin is that we learn the Torah!"

Reminders of the Torah . . .

The boy became quiet. Suddenly he noticed a fringe at the edge of his father's coat.

"And what are these?" he asked, pointing to the strings.

"Zizit," answered the father. "They are to remind us to follow the laws of the Torah."

"Every one seems to tell us to study the Torah, Father! I wish I could study it too!"

"You will, my son, very soon!"

Answer the questions to Topic II.

III. THE JEWISH SCHOOL

A year later the little boy was brought to school. He was five years old, and was bursting with eagerness to learn the Torah of which he had heard so much. Early one morning, Sonny and his father came to the synagogue not far from home. When they arrived, many other boys were already there. They were seated on the floor in a semi-circle. In front of them stood a bench. Some of the children were talking to their neighbors while others were reading from scrolls. They kept reading from the same scroll over and over, apparently memorizing their lesson. When the teacher entered, the pupils arose, and remained standing until he sat down on his bench, for the teacher was very much respected by his pupils. There was complete silence, from the moment he entered. His greeting, "Shalom, my children," was answered with "Shalom, respected teacher."

At this point the teacher noticed the boy's father,

and beckoned to him. Father approached and asked permission to enroll his boy. The teacher was glad to accept the new pupil and told them the rules concerning attendance at the school. The boy must come each morning except Saturday, and stay till after sundown. He would have to study all day with only a short period for lunch and rest. Father would have to pay a few silver shekels a year for his son's tuition. The father smiled sadly when he heard this condition, for he knew that the teacher could not earn a living from the tuition fees that the pupils paid and had to eke out his living by making shoes at night. He, therefore readily agreed to the conditions, and left his son in the school.

There were some 30 boys in the room, ranging in age from five to thirteen. The teacher's assistant, a young man, was on hand to help beginners and those who found it difficult to learn their lessons. He had a strap handy which he used whenever he found a pupil was not attending to his work.

Answer the questions to Topic III.

IV. WHAT THE CHILDREN LEARNED IN SCHOOL

The first lesson was reading. The little fellow was given a scroll on which the prayer "Shema" was written without the vowels which you have in your Siddur. The assistant read the prayer with him over and over and over again. The young teacher did not try to teach him the letters of the alphabet; he simply read and read and read the prayer until the boy had learned it by heart. Slowly, the lad began to realize that the first word was Shema. Then he noticed that it was composed of three letters, the first letter had the sound of sh, the second—ma, while the third letter was not sounded at all. In the same way, he learned that the second word, Yisroel, was also composed of a number of Hebrew letters, which, after a while, he learned to recognize. Some time passed before he was really able to read. By that time he had learned almost all the prayers by heart. He was then ready to learn to write.

His first lessons in writing were given him on wax tablets. With a pointed stick, he formed the square letters of the Hebrew alphabet in the wax. After a while, his father provided him with parchment (a thin sheet of sheepskin that looks like thick paper), ink, and a reed pen.

The boy was then given the opportunity which he had so long awaited. A scroll of the Torah was placed in his hands, and he began to study it, though he was barely six years old.

He spent almost the entire day in reading parts of the Torah and in re-reading them. The Torah was written in Hebrew, but that did not bother him. Hebrew was not difficult, because that was the language he spoke, just as we speak English. Of course he did not speak Hebrew perfectly. He made many errors in grammar, and often used Aramaic words instead of Hebrew. However, you must remember that not all American children speak English perfectly. The child's knowledge of Hebrew was enough for him to know the meanings of most of the words.

Nevertheless he found the study of the Bible difficult for the same reasons that you find an English translation of the Bible hard to understand. There are many teachings in the Torah, Nebiim, and Ketubim that are difficult even for adults. However, the boy was patient, and studied from eight to ten hours each day, for six days a week. On the seventh day, the lad attended the Sabbath morning services held in his synagogue, and in the afternoon he spent some time in reviewing the week's work. As a result of his steady work, the lad learned the contents of the Torah in about two years.

The boy took very little time for play or for any other studies, such as arithmetic, literature, or a foreign language. He did, however, take some time for exercise, especially swimming. He also learned a trade, such as weaving. Most of his day, however, was spent in the study of the Written Law. In time, he came to know the Torah very well, and began to think of the days when he would be able to attend the lectures given by the greatest rabbis of Jerusalem in the house of study known by its Hebrew name, Bet Midrash.

Answer the questions to Topic IV.

V. WHAT THE PALESTINIAN CHILDREN LEARNED OUTSIDE

The boy's education in home and school gave him a great love for thorough knowledge of the Torah. But the home and the school were not the only places where the boy learned to be truly Jewish. He learned it during his free time, too. Wherever he went, he found places which were holy and interesting. These places made him proud of his people and his country. Whenever he took a trip across Palestine on camel-back he found many a place where his ancestors had fought for their freedom. Some of these were marked by big piles of stones. He also saw graves where Jewish heroes lay buried, and remembered with a thrill how these men had died for their God and their people.

In wandering through the streets of Jerusalem, he saw many a synagogue, school, and Bet Midrash. When he observed the king's beautiful palace, he rejoiced that the Jews now had a ruler of their own, and were no longer governed by foreign kings. The sight of the Temple always made him happy and proud. He was glad that he and his people worshipped the great and almighty God. He was proud of his people because, though its Temple had been destroyed, its land robbed, and its cities burnt, it had returned to life again. No other people had teachers greater than Moses, prophets greater than Isaiah, and scholars greater than Simeon ben Shetah.

Most exciting were the days when Jews from every part of Palestine and from every other country in the world came to Jerusalem to bring sacrifices to the Temple. Three times a year they came—Passover, Shabuot, and Sukkot. The city was then so crowded that there were not enough houses or hotels. Many pitched their tents in the streets and in the market places of Jerusalem. The campers were not worried about blocking traffic, for there were no automobiles, street cars or the like, in those days. People used only camels, donkeys, or horses, and these animals were taught to watch their step.

On Shabuot, the Bikkurim (The Festival of First Fruits) procession was held. People came from every village, driving before them oxen whose horns were gilded and whose necks were wreathed with olive leaves and branches. Each man carried a basket, often a silver one, containing the first fruits of his fields. These were brought to the Temple and presented to the Kohanim and Levites. Any child following one of these processions was sure to learn the reasons for everything that took place, and then appreciate the greatness of the Book which guided his people. Passover and Sukkot were also beautifully observed and added to the lad's knowledge and interest.

Thus did the Pharisees teach the children. Can we consider their help to the Jews less valuable than that of the Sadducees?

Answer the questions to Topic V.

ADDITIONAL READING

The Unconquered. There are two stories in this book which will help you understand your lesson.

"There Was Once a Queen" tells about the queen sister of Simeon ben Shetah. The story begins on page 238.

"The Golden Ladder" tells about Simeon himself. It begins on page 246.

The Great March. There is a very fanciful story about Simeon ben Shetah told in this book entitled "Walking between Raindrops." It begins on page 30.

Great Men in Israel. This is a little book of stories of great Jewish leaders of whom we shall learn this year. It was written by Rabbi J. Max Weis.

Read the story "The King and the Judge," beginning on page 10.

SOMETHING TO THINK ABOUT

1. Very few girls went to school in the days of Simeon ben Shetah. Yet they knew all about the Jewish holidays and were acquainted with all Jewish customs. How did they get their knowledge?
2. While many Jewish boys now attend a Jewish school for only a few hours a week, boys formerly spent over 40 hours in their Jewish school. How many hours should one attend? Why?

What Brought Jewish Independence to an End?

WHILE the Pharisees devoted their energies to the service of God, the Sadducees worked for the benefit of the people in the land. As a result, the country became more prosperous and the people more pious. All might have been well, if they had been left to themselves. But the Romans at that time were eager to conquer the world, and little Palestine lay in their path. And so, once again, trouble visited our people. This time, the Jews lost everything they held dear. First their freedom was taken away, and then their Temple was burnt and Jerusalem utterly destroyed!

I. THE UNFORTUNATE QUARREL FOR THE CROWN

The story, telling how Jewish independence came to an end, begins with a quarrel. A few years after the Pharisee Simeon ben Shetah had introduced his system of compulsory education for children, the last of the Hasmonean rulers died. Two sons, Hyrcan and Aristobul, both wanted to become king. Now Hyrcan, the older brother, was a simple man who did not have the ability to rule, while the younger brother,

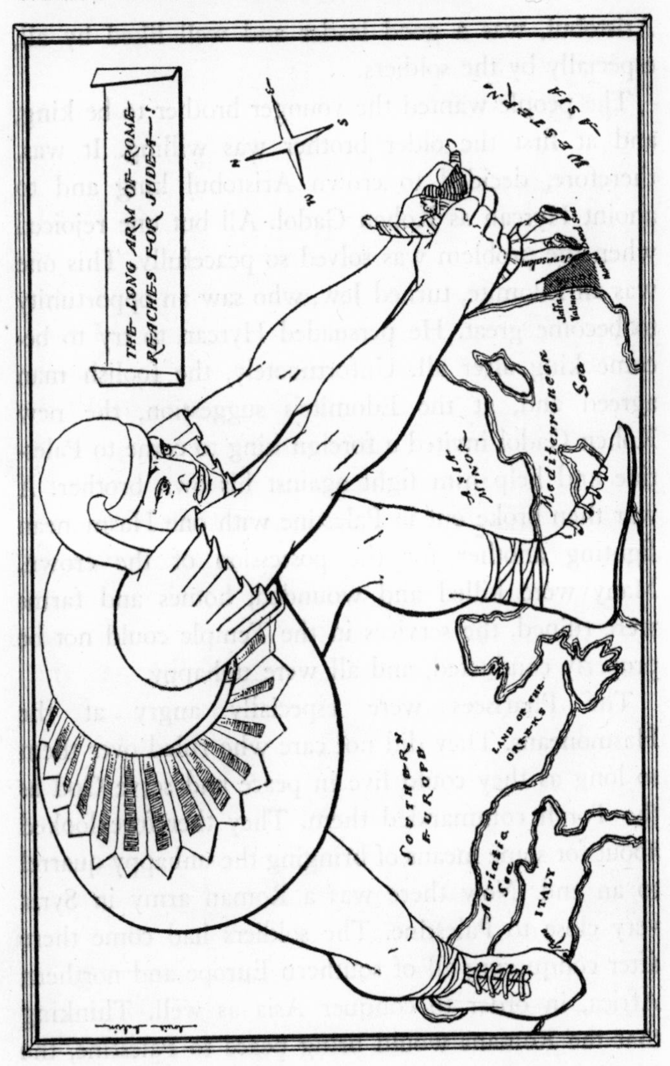
THE LONG ARM OF ROME
REACHES FOR JUDEA—!
WESTERN ASIA
ASIA MINOR
Mediterranean Sea
LAND OF THE GREEKS
SOUTHERN EUROPE
Adriatic Sea
ITALY

Aristobul, was a good leader and well liked by all, especially by the soldiers.

The people wanted the younger brother to be king, and at first the older brother was willing. It was, therefore, decided to crown Aristobul king and to anoint Hyrcan as Kohen Gadol. All but one rejoiced when the problem was solved so peacefully. This one was an Edomite, turned Jew, who saw an opportunity to become great. He persuaded Hyrcan to try to become king after all. Unfortunately, the foolish man agreed and, at the Edomite's suggestion, the new Kohen Gadol invited a foreign king to come to Palestine and help him fight against his own brother. A war then broke out in Palestine with one Hasmonean fighting another for the possession of the crown. Many were killed and wounded, homes and farms were ruined, the services in the Temple could not be properly conducted, and all were unhappy.

The Pharisees were especially angry at the Hasmoneans. They did not care who ruled over them so long as they could live in peace and serve God as the Torah commanded them. They therefore looked about for some means of bringing the unhappy quarrel to an end. Now there was a Roman army in Syria very close to Palestine. The soldiers had come there after conquering all of southern Europe and northern Africa, in order to conquer Asia as well. Thinking that the Romans would bring peace to Palestine, the Pharisees sent messengers to the Roman general, asking him to make their country part of the Roman empire and thus put an end to the war. At the same time, Hyrcan and Aristobul sent messengers to the general, asking him to choose one of them as king. The Roman was clever. He wanted to do as the Pharisees had asked, but he feared that taking over Palestine at once might mean war against an army of whose strength he was not certain and against a people of whose fierceness in war he had heard many a story. He therefore decided to use an old Roman trick—to divide the people and then rule over them. Accordingly, the Roman general chose the weak and foolish Hyrcan as king.

Answer the questions to Topic I of Chapter 10.

II. HOW PALESTINE LOST ITS INDEPENDENCE

What the general expected, now took place. Aristobul and his friends refused to accept the Roman's decision, while the friends of Hyrcan rejoiced in it. The Jews were divided into two distinct groups, one of which was friendly toward the Romans. The general took advantage of this situation at once. He quickly captured Aristobul and kept him prisoner in the Roman camp. When friends of the captured Hasmonean prepared to fight for him, the Roman general entered Palestine with a large army, defeated them, and put all their leaders to death. When the Jews angrily rose in revolt against Hyrcan, who had been crowned by the Romans, they were quickly defeated and large numbers of them were killed.

Soon afterward, a Roman official informed the

"victorious" Hyrcan that he was no longer king, but merely Kohen Gadol and leader of the Jewish people. He was granted only those rights which the Kohen Gadol had had in the days of the Persians, Greeks, Egyptians, and Syrians. Thus the Jews lost their independence.

Very few Jews, however, were ready to admit that the Romans were going to remain masters of Palestine for long. Time after time they rose in revolt but each time they met with defeat. In one of these revolts, Hyrcan was captured, exiled to a foreign land, and another Hasmonean was crowned king of the Jewish people. For a short time it seemed as if the Jews might retain their independence after all. Unfortunately, the Romans were determined to conquer Palestine and keep it as part of their Empire. The happiness of the people did not concern the Romans at all. They, therefore, picked Herod, the son of the evil Edomite, as king over the Jewish people and sent their armies into Palestine to force the Jews to accept him as their ruler. A fierce war broke out between the Jews, led by their new Hasmonean king, and the Romans, who supported Herod. The Roman soldiers again showed that they were too strong for the Jews and placed Herod on the throne.

Answer the questions to Topic II.

III. HOW HEROD RULED IN PALESTINE

As everyone expected, Herod, the evil son of the evil Edomite, did everything he could to keep the Romans as masters of Palestine. When he found a Jew unfriendly to the Romans, he ordered him executed. He collected heavy taxes and handed the money to the Romans. He raised a large army to put down any revolt which might arise, and to help the Romans whenever necessary. Herod even fought Roman enemies outside of Palestine. In addition, the "Jewish" king tried to make the Jews live like the Romans. He built cities to look like the Roman cities. He built arenas in which men fought against wild beasts or against other men, just as they did in Rome. On the very gates of the holy Temple he placed a golden eagle, which stood for Rome. In short, Herod did anything and everything to please the Romans, because he knew that only with their help could he remain king of the Jews.

Herod ruled over the Jews with an iron hand. Anyone who stood in his way was put to death. Members of his own family were treated no better. He executed his wife and had several of his children put to death. Relatives of his wife were assassinated. People were drowned, poisoned, or cast into dark, deep dungeons. Jews were imprisoned, driven out of the land, or put to death by the hundreds. A Roman general, hearing of Herod's cruelty, said that he would rather be a pig than a son of Herod.

You can imagine how much the Jews must have hated him! And yet he was their king. He knew well enough that the Jews hated him and would very much like to see him dead. This made him very uncomfort-

Only Kohanim and Levites worked on the new building.

able, for not even a Herod likes to be unpopular. He therefore began to think of doing something which would please the Jews as well as the Romans. He knew that if he should revolt against the Romans, the Jews would be very much pleased, but such an act would displease his friends and supporters, the Romans.

Answer the questions to Topic III.

IV. WHAT HEROD DID FOR THE JEWS

Two good ideas did come to Herod's mind. The first was to help Jewish merchants carry on trade with other countries. He gave the Roman emperor valuable presents and succeeded in getting him to protect Jewish merchants during their travels in foreign lands. This did please the Jews, especially those living outside of Palestine. His second idea was even better. The old Temple had been standing for the last five hundred years, and looked rather shabby. He decided to replace it by a big, beautiful house of worship. To do this, Herod trained the Kohanim and Levites in building, and had them put up the new Temple, which quickly became famous throughout the world. The Jews were particularly pleased because only Kohanim and Levites worked on the new building. It made them feel that the Temple was now truly holy. Moreover, care was taken not to tear down any part of the old Temple before the new one was built in its place. Thus, the worship of God went on without interruption while the new building was being erected.

Ordinarily, the builder of such a beautiful Temple would have won the heart of his people. But Herod could not. He had acted so cruelly toward the Jews, that they could never forgive him. They hated him to the very end, and rejoiced greatly at his death. They hoped that the next ruler would be better, and would help them regain the freedom which the Romans had taken away. Of one thing all Jews thought they were certain—the new king could not possibly be worse than Herod. But they were wrong. The son was like his father, except that he did nothing to please them.

Answer the questions to Topic IV.

V. HOW PALESTINE WAS RULED BY ROMAN GOVERNORS

In their desperation, a number of Jewish leaders asked the Roman emperor to remove the king and appoint a Roman governor in his place. They did not realize that this meant the total loss of their freedom. However, they soon learned the bitter truth. A Roman governor was appointed to take the place of Herod's son. He governed Palestine even worse than had Herod and his son. His chief interest in Palestine was money. The happiness of the people did not concern him; whether the Jews liked him or did not was of no importance to him. He devoted most of his time to the task of getting more and more money for himself and the Roman emperor. The taxes were heavy but still they did not bring in enough money to satisfy him.

The governor was all the more anxious to get as much money as possible because he knew that his job would last for only a few years. He therefore began to use the same methods as had Antiochus. He stole the Temple treasures when he could. He appointed as officers over the Jews only those who gave him large sums of money as bribes. Even the position of Kohen Gadol was sold to the one who paid most. When the Jews objected, the governor paid no attention. When they took to arms, the Roman soldiers fell upon them and massacred them.

The Jews were in a desperate position. Their freedom was gone. But they did not lose hope. Encouraged by their leaders, they still believed that a day would yet come when they would succeed in driving the hated Romans out of Palestine, and live there in peace and happiness.

Many hundreds of years have passed since that time. But the Jews have not yet rebuilt Palestine. The Romans were indeed driven out, but not by the Jews. For centuries the land was neglected and sank more and more into ruin. During the past fifty years tremendous efforts have been made by Jews to upbuild the land. In that upbuilding all Jews should be interested. In future years you will learn how to aid in this great task.

Answer the questions to Topic V.

ADDITIONAL READING

The Unconquered. The Roman general who conquered Palestine was Pompey. His notions about Jews and their religion show how little people knew about us in those days. Read "Pompey's Discovery," beginning on page 267.

Great Jews since Bible Times. Mrs. Elma Ehrlich Levinger is the author of this easy little book. Read "Herod, the Builder of the Temple" on pages 10–12.

SOMETHING TO THINK ABOUT

1. Were the Pharisees right in asking the Romans to make Palestine part of the Roman Empire? Why?
2. Why did Herod try more than the Roman governors to please the Jews?
3. Herod helped to improve the business of the Jewish merchants and rebuilt the Temple. Which of these two accomplishments pleased the Sadducees most? Which pleased the Pharisees most? Which is most important in your eyes? Why?

Who Took Over the Leadership?

DURING all the years in which Herod and the Roman governors ruled over the Jews, the people longed for two things. They wanted to know the Torah and to be free of Rome. The rulers well knew what the people wished, but refused to help them. On the contrary, they did all they could to keep Palestine under Roman control. And as for helping the Jews to live in accordance with the laws of the Torah, the rulers did not know how. So, though the people obeyed them, they had neither love nor respect for them. They did not consider these men their leaders, for true leaders help their people to attain their desires.

The people, therefore, turned to their Pharisee teachers for guidance. Especially did they respect the heads of the great colleges in Jerusalem, where men spent their days and nights studying the Torah. As their confidence in the king and his Kohen Gadol decreased their faith in their teachers grew stronger.

1. HOW HILLEL BECAME A JEWISH LEADER

In the reign of Herod, which began about 1975 years ago, a learned teacher who came from Babylonia was elected head of a great college and became the true leader of his people. Unlike the king or his Kohen Gadol, this man, called Hillel, neither killed nor bribed any one in order to reach his high position. Indeed, he was the most peaceful soul in Palestine; he won his place so quietly that Herod did not even try to murder him! And you know of course, what Herod did to any one whom he suspected of wanting to be a leader of the Jewish people.

Hillel became leader by winning the hearts of his people. They admired him for many reasons. He was more learned in the Torah than any lawyer in the laws of his land, and he knew the Jewish customs and ways of living better than any other man; and no wonder! Very few people nowadays *can* or *do* study as many hours each day, as many days each year, and as many years of their lives, as did the learned men at the time when the Second Temple stood in Jerusalem. And Hillel studied even more diligently than the others.

Answer the questions to Topic I of Chapter 11.

II. HOW HILLEL WAS EDUCATED

At six, Hillel was already attending school from early morning until sundown, six days of the week. On the Sabbath, he rested by reviewing all the lessons which he had learned during the week. That is how Jewish children studied in those days.

As he grew older, Hillel realized that the Babylonian Jews were not learned enough. He therefore journeyed to Palestine, where the best teachers were to be found. Hillel was very poor, and had to earn his living by chopping trees and peddling firewood. He earned very little; yet each day he paid half of his earnings to the college doorkeeper as the price for his admission. This payment left him with hardly enough to buy bread, but Hillel never stayed away from school. Food was not as important to him as learning.

There is a story which tells how much Hillel desired to study, and how little he cared about his comfort. One wintry afternoon, when he came to the college, he had no money for the doorkeeper. He was not admitted. But that did not stop Hillel. He climbed up to the skylight, put his ear close to the glass and listened. He became so absorbed in following the lesson that he did not notice how cold it was getting. Snow began to fall; but the flakes did not disturb Hillel, for his eyes and ears were fixed on his teachers. He would have frozen to death had not someone noticed that the room had become darker than usual. Some of the pupils climbed to the roof, where they found Hillel, unconscious. They lifted him up, carried him into the schoolroom, and nursed him back to life. After that, Hillel was always admitted without charge.

Hillel now spent more time than ever before at his studies. One important reason for his devotion to the Torah was the realization that it helped him to be truly religious. When anyone said to him: "I am too busy to study just now," Hillel answered: "Unless you begin now, you are not likely to study later."

After many years of hard work, Hillel knew as

Hillel—the Great Teacher.

much as his teachers. But that did not satisfy him, for he kept right on studying. After the death of his teachers, Hillel became known as the most learned man in Palestine. This reputation was in itself enough to win for him the respect of all the Jewish people.

Answer the questions to Topic II.

III. WHY THE PEOPLE LOVED HILLEL

But learned as Hillel was, he was still very patient with people who were stupid or mean. It was said that no one had ever seen him lose his temper. There is a story of a man who bet another that he could make Hillel angry. To win this bet, he went to Hillel's home one Friday afternoon when Hillel was busy with his preparations for the Sabbath. The man went into the house and shouted,

"Hillel, Oh, Hillel, where are you?"

Hillel appeared and asked, "What is it, my son?"

The man was surprised at the mildness of Hillel's tone, but he went on:

"Why do Babylonians have round heads?"

It was a foolish question, and was meant to be insulting, for Hillel himself was a Babylonian. However, Hillel answered quietly:

"I suppose that the Babylonian nurses do not know how to take care of children."

The man left. Hillel went back to prepare for the Sabbath. Suddenly the man came in again.

"Hillel, Oh, Hillel," he called. "Where are you?" Hillel came in again and asked:

"What can I do for you, my son?" The man asked another foolish question.

"Why do many Africans have flat feet?"

Hillel did not lose his patience. Instead, he told the man that they had flat feet because they often walked on soft ground. The man was shocked. He had never believed that any one quite like Hillel existed. He left, but soon returned. This time he said:

"I hope there are no more Hillels in this world."

Hillel was amused at the man's words and asked why.

"On account of you, I lost a bet!" the man cried. Thereupon Hillel said,

"That's too bad, but I still believe that it is better that you should lose a bet than that anyone should lose his temper."

Many similar stories are told about Hillel. A non-Jew once came to him and said:

"I have just seen the Kohen Gadol dressed in the most beautiful robes I have ever seen. I want to become a Jew so that I may be appointed Kohen Gadol and wear gorgeous garments, as he does."

Hillel was displeased. He wanted people to become Jews in order to worship God and learn His Torah, and not so that they might wear beautiful clothes. But he did not drive the man from his house. Instead, he began to teach him those laws of the Torah which set forth who might become Kohen Gadol and what his duties were. The man became so interested in the Torah that he forgot about his wish to become Kohen

Gadol. He became a Jew and resolved to study more of the Torah.

At another time a man came to Hillel and said: "I should like to become a Jew, but I am too busy to learn the Torah. If you can teach it to me while I stand on one foot, then I am willing to become a Jew. If you cannot I shall continue to be an idol worshipper."

Most of us would have laughed at such a foolish request; or we might have become angry, for it is quite impossible to teach the Torah so quickly. However, Hillel was not like most of us. He neither laughed nor became angry. This is what he said to the man:

"The most important idea in the Torah is, 'What is hateful to thee, *do not* unto others.' Everything else which you will find in the Torah is merely an explanation of this sentence."

The man was pleased. He became a Jew and studied the Torah to learn the explanations.

In addition to being a great scholar and a very patient man, Hillel did much to make other people happy. He was very kind to the poor and tried to give them some comfort. One day his wife heard that a newly married couple were too poor to buy a good dinner for their wedding feast. She gave them the meal she had prepared for her own husband. When Hillel came home, he had to wait while his wife prepared another meal for him. When he heard the reason for the delay, he praised his wife for her kindness.

When people spoke to him about the wrongs and

sins of others, Hillel advised them not to be too sure of wickedness in other people. He felt that no one had the right to consider another bad or sinful until he had taken the trouble to find out what had made him do wrong.

If a man came to Hillel for help, he received prompt and generous assistance. One man had been so rich that, when he rode on his horse, he had been in the habit of paying several men to run in front of him to clear the way. When the rich man lost his fortune, Hillel sometimes hired men to do that for him to make him forget his poverty. One day, because Hillel was unable to hire any one to do it, Hillel himself ran before the man.

One so thoughtful was bound to make friends and win respect. It is small wonder then that Hillel, who was a great scholar, a very patient man, and a noble soul, should have won the love and respect of all Jews. He was a true leader and teacher.

Answer the questions to Topic III.

IV. HILLEL MAKES NEW LAWS

So highly was Hillel thought of that his word was obeyed more readily than any law issued by the king or Kohen Gadol. No policemen were needed to enforce any of his decisions. His opinions were accepted as part of the "Oral Law." One "Oral Law" issued by Hillel is especially interesting.

There is a law in the Torah which says that with the arrival of the Seventh Year, known as the Sabbatical Year, loans made in previous years need not be repaid. As a result, no one was willing to lend money a year or two before the Seventh Year. Business men who honestly intended to repay the loans were unable to secure the money they needed for conducting their affairs. Hillel therefore issued his famous "Oral Law" to overcome the difficulty. He declared that the court might be permitted to collect a loan during or after the Seventh Year, even though the lender himself might not do so. Then people who wanted to borrow money, simply handed the court a note asking it to collect the money when the debt was due.

Note how wise Hillel was in handling this problem. He did not declare that the Written Law of the Bible was wrong. Like a good Pharisee, he believed that every law in the Bible was holy and should be obeyed. However, he realized that the purpose of the law was to protect the poor Jews who could not repay personal loans, and had nothing to do with loans made for business reasons. He, therefore, added the Oral Law to make the Written Law clear to all.

Hillel added many more Oral Laws. And each time, Hillel's laws proved helpful to the people, who obeyed them gladly. Naturally, they loved and admired their great leader and teacher. They said that he was a descendant of King David. We do not know whether Hillel really was a prince by birth, but we do know that he was a prince in learning and a king in character. Hillel fully deserved the confidence, respect, and love of his people. When he died, some 1900 years ago, the Jews mourned his death as deeply as they would have mourned the death of a father.

Answer the questions to Topic IV.

ADDITIONAL READING

The Unconquered. There are three stories in this book that you will enjoy reading: "The Boy on the Roof" pages 278–287; "Crassus in Jerusalem" pages 288–299; "Losers, Winners" pages 300–308.

The Great March. Here is another set of three stories that you might read: "School on the Roof," pages 35–39; "The Bet" pages 40–43; "Torah on One Foot," pages 44–45.

Great Men in Israel. Read "A Prince with Two Crowns," pages 13–17; "Gentle Hillel," pages 18–20.

Great Jews since Bible Times. Read "Hillel the Poor Student" pages 7–9.

SOMETHING TO THINK ABOUT

1. Why did Hillel issue Oral Laws to explain the Written Law of the Torah, instead of changing the Biblical Law?
2. Some of the great Jews of whom you learned in this book are: Ezra, Nehemiah, Haggai, Zechariah and Judah Maccabee. In what way does each one resemble Hillel?

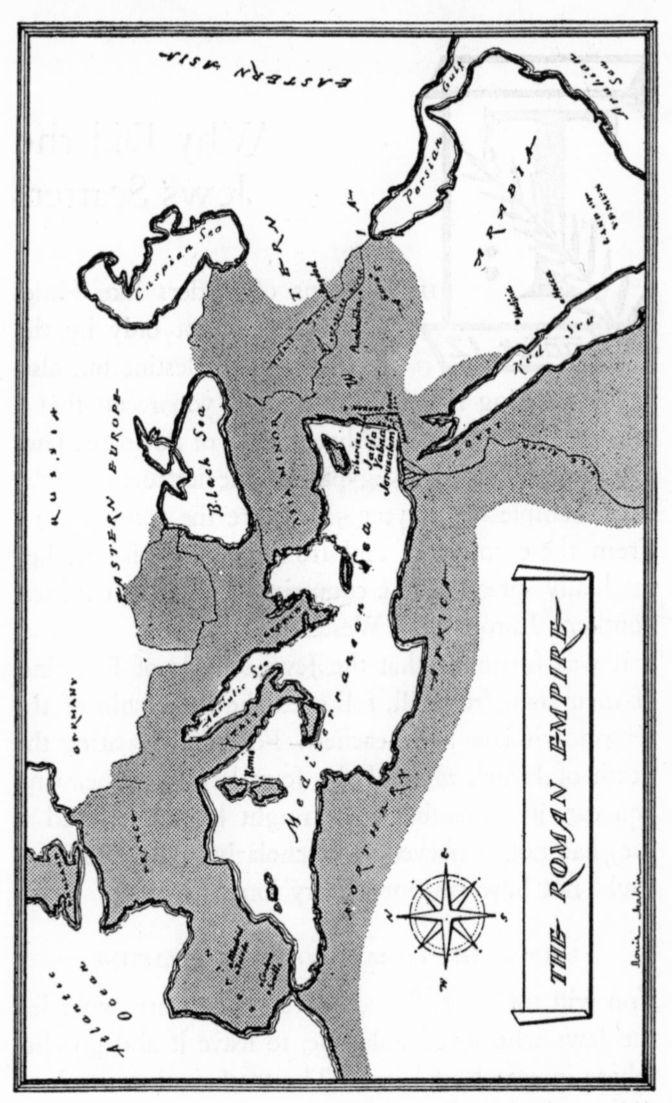
THE ROMAN EMPIRE
EASTERN ASIA
Caspian Sea
Black Sea
EASTERN EUROPE
RUSSIA
GERMANY
Adriatic Sea
Mediterranean Sea
ASIA MINOR
ARABIA
Persian Gulf
Red Sea
Arabian Sea
Tiberias
Jaffa
Yabneh
Jerusalem
Rome
Medina
Mecca
Atlantic Ocean

Why Did the Jews Scatter?

THE opinions of leaders like Hillel were accepted not only by the Jews living in Palestine but also by those living in other lands. And you recall that a great number of Jews *did* live outside of Palestine. Jews had lived in Persia and Egypt since the destruction of the First Temple in the year 586 before the common era. From these countries and from Palestine itself, they gradually spread to the countries of Northern Africa, Southern Europe, and Western Asia.

It was fortunate that the Jews outside of Palestine, of their own free will, followed the leadership of the Jewish scholars and teachers. For, shortly after the death of Hillel, *most* of the Jews left Palestine. And you can just imagine what might have happened if they had not all obeyed their scholarly leaders! Judaism could not have continued very long!

I. HOW THE ROMANS GOVERNED PALESTINE

You will undoubtedly be interested to learn what led the Jews who loved Palestine, to leave it and go elsewhere in search of homes. The truth is that the Jews did not do it willingly. They were forced to leave.

The story is a very sad one. It was first told by a Jew who lived at that time—Josephus. This man wrote a book that you may still read in its original Greek if you can, or in English. It is called "Concerning the Jewish War." The title itself will give you an idea of what happened at that time. Nor is it difficult to guess what brought on the war.

The Roman governors who came to Palestine not only failed to help the Jews, but actually made it harder for them to live happily. They were interested in just two things:

1. Getting rich quickly. It did not matter to the governor how he obtained his money—whether it was by collecting taxes, by accepting bribes, or by stealing the treasures of the Temple. No method for getting rich was considered too mean by some of the Roman governors. They knew that they would not hold their office for long, and so they tried to get as much as they could in as short a time as possible.

2. Keeping "peace" in Palestine. The governors knew that the people in Palestine were very unhappy and might revolt at any time. They were therefore constantly spying on the Jews to make sure that no one would arise to lead them against the Romans. Any person accused of being an enemy of Rome was put to death by the cruel Roman method of nailing him to a large wooden cross. This punishment was known as "crucifixion." Thus, when the Jew, Joshua, better known as Jesus, called himself a Messiah, he was suspected by the Roman governor of trying to free his

people from the Romans. Therefore, the governor ordered Jesus to be nailed to a cross. Some people, later on, said that the Jews themselves had crucified Jesus. But we know that the Jews had no power to put anyone to death in those days, and never in all their history did they put any one to death by crucifixion.

After Jesus had died on the cross, a few of his friends still insisted that he was the true Messiah. Most Jews, of course, did not believe them. But the few who did, taught others to believe that Jesus was the true Messiah and that he would save all who believed in him. Many people, whom we call Christians, then began to worship Jesus as if he were God. They called him Christ, which is a Greek word meaning Messiah. In this way a new religion, called Christianity, arose.

The new religion was easier to keep than the Jewish religion, and it was much finer than idol-worshipping which most non-Jews still practiced. Christianity, therefore, spread quickly among the Europeans. At present almost all the people of Europe and America are Christians. The Jewish people, however, could never believe that the Jew, Joshua, was a Messiah, and they could not accept the new religion.

Besides Joshua, there were others who believed themselves Messiahs and were treated with equal harshness by the Romans. One man was so sure that he was a Messiah, that he promised to perform a miracle to prove it. He said that he would split the waters of the Jordan, cross the river without a boat, and come out on the other side, perfectly dry. Some Jews believed him, and followed him to the banks of the Jordan, to watch him perform this miracle. However, when the Roman governor found out about this new Messiah, he sent a troop of soldiers who overtook him before he reached the river and killed him on the spot. The Romans did not want any Messiah to come and save the Jews. In this way Roman governors kept "peace" in Palestine.

Answer the questions to Topic I of Chapter 12.

II. HOW THE JEWS FELT ABOUT THE ROMAN RULE

The people hated the Roman governors and their methods of keeping "peace." Some of them began to plan revolt. Such plans had to be kept secret, for if the Romans had found out about them, the leaders would have been immediately put to death. But despite the secrecy, large numbers of men joined the plot to revolt against Rome. These revolutionaries, called Zealots, felt that they could drive out the Romans in the same way as the Hasidim had driven out the Syrians. In spite of the danger of being caught by the Romans, they met often to plan the details of the revolt.

Many of our people realized how difficult it would be for them to defeat the Romans, and gave up all hope of freedom. They took no interest in the plans of the Zealots and merely prayed that God would send His Messiah soon to save them from further trouble.

As might have been expected, most of the people were not altogether without hope. They were patriots

Josephus had continued his studies in one of the colleges in Jerusalem.

who loved their God, and their country; but they knew very well that it was next to impossible to drive the Romans out of Palestine. These men, therefore, refused to join the Zealots, but they did not simply sit back and watch the Romans mistreat the Jews. They constantly sent requests to the Romans, urging them to rule the people justly, to let them study their Torah in peace, and allow them to live in accordance with their religion.

Answer the questions to Topic II.

III. HOW THE REVOLT BEGAN

To this latter group, Josephus belonged. He was interested in studies rather than in war. As a lad, he had attended school and studied Torah under Pharisee teachers. When he became older, Josephus had continued his studies in one of the colleges in Jerusalem. From his Pharisee teachers, Josephus had learned the Oral as well as the Written Law. He had also studied Greek and Latin and thus learned a great deal about the Greeks and the Romans.

When he was about twenty-five years old, Josephus visited Rome, and saw the strength and power of the Roman people. He was impressed by their great wealth, their beautiful buildings, and their mighty armies. During the short time that he stayed in Rome, he realized how utterly impossible it would be for the Jews to free themselves from Rome. Yet, when he returned to Palestine, he determined to help the Zealots fight the Romans.

There were several reasons for Josephus' decision. In the first place, the heavy taxes which the Romans had levied upon the Jews had made them so miserably poor that a great many had had to sell their farms and go to the cities to find work. If there was no work, they were forced either to starve or steal.

Secondly, the Roman governors took it upon themselves to appoint the Kohen Gadol, just as Antiochus had done in the days of the Maccabees. The man who paid the highest price was appointed Kohen Gadol whether or not he was fit for the honor.

Thirdly, the Roman governors did not treat the people fairly. One of them put a golden eagle on the gates of the holy Temple. The Jews felt that the eagle on the gates of their Temple was almost as bad as an idol within their Temple, and asked him to remove it. The Roman governor forced the committee of Jews that came to him, to wait outside for several days before he finally allowed them to speak to him; and he yielded only when he realized that these men would rather die in battle than have the eagle on the Temple gates.

Once, Greeks and Jews living in one of the cities of Palestine quarrelled. The Roman soldiers attacked the Jews and killed many of them. When a committee of Jews came to the governor to complain, they were thrown into prison.

One day, the governor ordered the Kohen Gadol to give him a large sum of money from the Temple treasury. When the people learned of this order, they became very angry and many of them made fun of the governor by going about the streets with cups in their hands, begging charity for the Roman governor. To punish these men, the governor ordered a troop of Roman soldiers to attack them. A large number of Jews were killed. To make sure that the Romans would always be masters of Jerusalem, an additional troop of Roman soldiers came to the city on the following day. The Jews were ordered to greet the soldiers respectfully, and did so. But the Romans did not return the greeting. This insult angered the Jews, and a number of Zealots began throwing stones at the soldiers. A fight followed, during which the Jews drove the Romans out of the city.

Answer the questions to Topic III.

IV. THE SAD ENDING OF THE WAR

This fight was the beginning of the revolt against Rome. Josephus felt that all self-respecting Jews should join the Zealots and try as hard as possible to drive the cruel Romans out of Palestine. For a while, he forgot the utter impossibility of defeating the Romans. He was determined to fight them, and, like the Maccabees, he hoped to drive the enemy out of Palestine. This happened about 1850 years ago.

The leaders of the revolt were glad to have the help of Josephus, and appointed him a general, although he was hardly thirty years old. He was given command of the Jewish army in the northern district of Palestine. This was the part first attacked by the Roman soldiers.

Josephus and his men fought bravely and, for a while, held off the enemy. However, Josephus was just a young man, with no previous experience in fighting, while the Roman troops were led by their ablest general. In spite of Josephus' efforts and the bravery of his men, the Romans finally succeeded in defeating him and destroying his army. Josephus now saw, once and for all, that the Jews stood no chance against the powerful Roman armies, and he surrendered. But his soldiers died rather than accept defeat.

The Roman general treated Josephus well and permitted him to do as he pleased. In return for this favor, Josephus went about Palestine, in the company of the Roman general, advising the defenders of each city to surrender to the Roman army. His efforts pleased the Romans but earned him the hatred of his fellow-Jews who considered him a coward and a traitor. Josephus was with the Romans when they finally reached Jerusalem and laid siege to the city. He saw how the water and food supplies were cut off. Daily he could see how the people of Jerusalem who died of hunger, thirst, and disease, were thrown into a pit outside the walls of the city. But the defenders of the city did not give up. The Romans then put up battering rams and broke through one of the walls, only to find that another wall had been built behind it. The siege lasted for more than a year. Finally, the Romans climbed over the walls of Jerusalem, and killed those who were defending the city. But there were more Jewish soldiers in the fort surrounding the Temple. The Romans at-

. . . they set fire to the Temple!

tacked them too. In the year 70, on the ninth day of the Jewish month of Ab, the Romans broke into the fort, set fire to the Temple, and, after a hard struggle, captured the leaders of the revolt. In Hebrew, this sad day is called Tisha (the ninth) b'Ab (in the month of Ab). It is still observed as a day of mourning.

Palestine was now almost completely under the control of the Romans. Practically every city and fortress was in their hands. The Temple was burned; the land was desolate. Yet a number of Zealots still held the fortress in Masada and refused to surrender. It took three years to destroy this last fortress and leave Palestine completely conquered. Much of the land was given away to Roman soldiers and the city of Jerusalem was almost completely destroyed. Most of those left alive after this terrible war, fled to other countries. Many went to Persia, a large number escaped to Asia Minor and the southern coast of Europe, while others went to Egypt and the countries on the northern coast of Africa. From those countries Jews gradually became scattered all over the world. Today there is practically no country in the world without Jews.

Answer the questions to Topic IV.

V. THE WORK OF JOSEPHUS

When at last the war was over, Josephus, too, decided to leave Palestine and go to Rome. Many Jews were living there. Many had been brought as captives and sold as slaves. Others had come there to carry on business. Most of them, however, were unhappy and suffered from the hatred of the Romans, who considered them queer. They did not work on the Sabbath, worshipped a God that could not be seen, and practised ceremonies that were altogether different from those of the Romans. Josephus felt that if the Romans could only be made to understand Jewish life, they would treat the Jews better. He was strengthened in this belief by the fact that some of the more intelligent people admired the Jewish religion and not a few actually became Jews. He, therefore, wrote a history of the Jewish people from earliest times up to the time when the Jews began their war against the Romans. He wrote the book in Greek so that all learned Romans could read it for themselves and understand why the Jews lived in a manner which was so different from that of all other people known to the Romans.

When he finished this history, Josephus wrote two other important books. One described the last wars of the Jews against the Syrians and Romans. The other defended the Jews against foolish accusations of an Egyptian called Apion, who had written that the Jews worshipped a donkey and were unkind to strangers.

The books, written by Josephus, have come down to us. They describe the life of the Jews and their struggle for freedom better than any other book written in those days. In fact, they are the only good Jewish history books that were written so long ago. The Bible, of course, contains many historical facts, but it deals more with religion and literature than with history.

The Jews today still look upon Josephus as a traitor,

who, like Benedict Arnold, betrayed his people. However, we must remember that the Jews had not a chance to succeed in their fight against the Romans, and that no matter how much Josephus might have helped them with his sword, he actually did accomplish a great deal more for the Jews with his pen. Accordingly, we now remember Josephus more as a historian than as a traitor. His books are still read with interest by people wishing to know what happened in the early days of Jewish life.

Answer the questions to Topic V.

ADDITIONAL READING

The Unconquered. Pontius Pilate was a Roman governor. Jesus was brought before him for trial and condemned to death. You can learn about his character by reading: "Mightier Than the Sword," on page 309.

People in those times were greatly excited about the Messiah who was expected to arrive at that time and save his people from the Roman Governors. Read "How Is That Possible?" on page 319, and "The False Messiah" on page 329.

Great Jews since Bible Times. "The Pen and the Sword" is, as you must already know, a story about Josephus. It begins on page 19.

SOMETHING TO THINK ABOUT

1. Did Josephus harm the Jews when he accompanied the Roman army? If so, why? If not, why not?
2. Were the Jews right in rebelling against Rome?

How Did the Religious Leaders Unite the Jewish People?

When the war with Rome finally came to its sad end, the Jews were left without a land. They became a people without a home, a king, or a council, and without a Temple in which to worship God. The large majority of Jews now dwelt outside of Palestine; they lived in constant fear of attacks from their neighbors, who disliked them because they were different. What prevented them from giving up their religion and becoming like the people in whose midst they were living?

Credit for keeping the people loyal to Judaism belongs to the religious teachers who had been the true leaders ever since the time of the Hasmoneans. The outstanding rabbi of those days, Yohanan ben Zakkai, was especially helpful. Let us study his life and learn what he did.

I. HOW A SCHOOL WAS OPENED AT YABNEH

Yohanan, the son of Zakkai, lived at the same time as the historian Josephus. He, too, was an eye-witness of the war between his people and Rome. Long before Jerusalem was captured, he knew, as well as Josephus, that the Romans would defeat the Jews and destroy the city. He decided to do everything he could to save his people. And what do you think he did? Went out and fought the Romans? No! Organized a secret society? No! Yohanan built a little school in a small village in Palestine!

How did he expect a school to save his people? This is a long story. First, let us learn how he happened to build it. Yohanan lived in Jerusalem during the war. At the time when he decided to build his school, the city was surrounded by Romans, and Jewish sentinels always guarded the gates and allowed no one to go out or come in. They were afraid of traitors and Roman spies. Even Yohanan was not permitted to leave the city.

What could he do? The wise rabbi soon discovered a way. He knew that the dead were buried *outside* the city, and that funeral processions often passed through the gates of Jerusalem. Yohanan decided to make use of this knowledge. He called in a few of his students, explained his plan, and asked them to help. They agreed.

On the following day, some of his pupils announced that their teacher had died. No one doubted the truth of the report, as people were dying in Jerusalem by the hundreds. A little later, a sad group of Yohanan's pupils appeared at one of the gates of the city carrying a coffin in which lay their master. The soldiers, believing that Yohanan was dead, allowed the young men to leave Jerusalem with the coffin. Once they were out-

. . . a sad group of Yohanan's pupils appeared at one of the gates of the city carrying a coffin.

side the city, and beyond the sight of the soldiers guarding the gate, Yohanan went directly to the tent of the Roman general.

The general, who had previously heard that Yohanan ben Zakkai had advised his people against the war, was glad to meet him. What the Jew said to the Roman we do not know. Some people tell the following story about the meeting that took place in the general's tent. The rabbi greeted the general as if he were the Roman Emperor. When the general asked why he so honored him, Yohanan replied that the Romans would soon elect him emperor. At that very moment, a messenger arrived in camp and announced that the general had been chosen emperor of Rome. Imagine how happy the Roman was! No longer would he have to live on the battlefields. He could now dwell peacefully in Rome, and rule over most of the world. To the old Jew who first called him emperor, the Roman was very grateful and promised to grant him any request he might make. Yohanan then asked the newly-chosen emperor not to destroy the little town of Yabneh on the coast of the Mediterranean Sea and to permit him to conduct a school there. The Roman general immediately granted this simple request, and promised to do no harm to Yabneh or to the people living there. The general, of course, never knew that his promise helped the Jews to live long after Rome itself had been destroyed.

As soon as he received the permission of the Roman general, Yohanan, accompanied by several of his students, went to Yabneh and opened a school for the study of the Written and Oral Law. By the time the Romans had captured Jerusalem and destroyed the Temple, Yohanan already had the beginnings of a great school to which some of the most learned men of Palestine came. He then became known by the honorable title "Tanna," meaning, teacher.

When the sad news of the fall of Jerusalem and the destruction of the Temple reached the scholars in Yabneh, they mourned bitterly although they had expected it to happen. They wept over the many who had lost their lives and over the Temple, now a heap of ashes. Tisha b'Ab was proclaimed a day of sorrow for all Jews. To this day, many Jews fast on Tisha b'Ab, and recite sorrowful prayers.

Answer the questions to Topic I of Chapter 13.

II. HOW A NEW SANHEDRIN WAS ORGANIZED

The victory of the Romans brought the Tanna Yohanan face to face with a problem. The burning of the Temple made it impossible for Jews to worship God by bringing Him sacrifices as they had done for hundreds of years before. The destruction of Jerusalem broke up the Sanhedrin which had been making the Oral Laws that guided not only the Jews of Palestine but also those who lived outside that land. How were the people to worship God now that the Temple was gone? Who could now make laws that all the Jews would feel bound to obey?

The Tanna answered both these serious questions

with the help of the school in Yabneh. He first organized the wisest and most learned of his pupils into a council, which he called the Sanhedrin. (We must remember that his pupils were all grown up men and not children. His school was really a college.) Yohanan then announced that thereafter, the Yabneh Sanhedrin would make laws in the same way as had the old Sanhedrin in Jerusalem. The new Sanhedrin declared that, to worship God, it was no longer necessary to bring sacrifices in the Temple. Instead of sacrifices, the Jews were directed to show kindness to others, to act honestly, and to play fair. (Many prophets had said the same thing hundreds of years before.)

The Sanhedrin added that now all should pray to God as regularly as they had once brought sacrifices to the Temple.

Answer the questions to Topic II.

III. HOW THE SYNAGOGUE REPLACED THE TEMPLE

The Tanna and the Sanhedrin had no way of forcing the people to obey them. But so highly were they respected that most Jews obeyed Rabbi Yohanan and his Sanhedrin of their own free will. Observant Jews everywhere organized synagogues and attended them regularly now that they could no longer worship God by letting the Kohanim bring sacrifices for them. As a result, the Kohanim ceased being the leaders and servants of their people. The teachers and rabbis then became the leaders, and the synagogue took the place of the Temple.

To this day we can still see in our synagogue some of the ceremonies which used to be followed in the Temple. For instance, the Shofar (Ram's horn) is blown on Rosh Hashanah and on the evening which ends the Yom Kippur fast. On Sukkot men carrying the Lulab and Ethrog (the Palm Branch and Citron) march about the synagogue in the same way as they used to circle around the altar in the Temple.

In many synagogues, a booth is erected on the platform and children bring up gifts of fruits and flowers as was the custom when the Temple still stood in Jerusalem.

So well did the synagogue replace the Temple that the people learned to worship God better than ever before. *Each* person now felt obliged to take part in the services. Each one therefore learned to read and, incidentally, took the opportunity to study the Bible more carefully. The synagogue thus held the Jews closer to God and His Torah, and the custom of killing animals as sacrifices to God came to an end.

Thus, with the aid of the school in Yabneh, did the Tanna Yohanan hold the Jews together and teach them to live in accordance with the laws and customs of Judaism.

Before long, other problems arose. How were the people to know when to hold the festivals, since they had no written calendar? How were the festivals to be observed, now that they had no Temple? What should they do with the gifts usually given to the Temple?

These were only a few of the questions that concerned the Jews at that time. The Tanna Yohanan discussed these matters with the Sanhedrin. They studied the Written Law, and recalled the Oral Law that dealt with these problems. The decisions were then announced to the people. These announcements became part of the Oral Law. As the years passed, more and more decisions were added to the Oral Law which the people were expected to obey.

Answer the questions to Topic III.

IV. WHAT GAVE YOHANAN POWER OVER HIS PEOPLE?

You may wonder why the people so readily obeyed the Tanna. Here are some of the reasons. Yohanan was known to have studied under Hillel and was considered his best pupil. He was so devoted to the study of the Torah that people said no one ever came to the Bet Ha-midrash (the house of study) before Yohanan, and no one ever left it after him. Nor did anyone ever see him in the school when he was not studying some holy book.

So widely known was the reputation of Yohanan ben Zakkai, that even the Jews living outside of Palestine kept asking him questions about the correct meanings of the laws of the Torah. These he willingly answered, and had the satisfaction of seeing his explanations obeyed as if they were laws. His answers to questions, as well as those given by the Anshe Keneset Ha-gedolah and the Sanhedrin in Jerusalem, were added to the "Oral Law" and were followed by all.

Yohanan sent his pupils to distant cities; . . .

Jews living outside of Palestine were as eager to obey the Oral Law as those who remained in the land of their fathers. To help them, Yohanan sent his pupils to distant cities where they became rabbis and teachers. In this way, knowledge of the Torah and Oral Law spread among all Jews, and helped them remain loyal to Judaism even though the Romans had destroyed Jerusalem and had burnt the Temple.

As time passed, more Oral Laws were made by the Tannaim who followed Yohanan. After 150 years, there were so many such laws, that the greatest Tanna living at that time collected and arranged them in a special book, which we now call the Mishnah. Rabbis, later on, studied the laws found in the Mishnah and added many more. Three hundred years after the completion of the Mishnah, these laws were also collected and called Gemara. These two, the Mishnah and the Gemara (a Hebrew word meaning "learning"), are called "Talmud." We shall, in our later chapters, learn a good deal more about this interesting collection, and the men who were responsible for it.

Answer the questions to Topic IV.

ADDITIONAL READING

Prayerbook. Sayings of Rabbi Yohanan ben Zakkai are found among the "Sayings of the Fathers." Read Yohanan's most famous sayings in the *Union Prayerbook* at the bottom of page 153 and the top of page 154. In the *Authorized Daily Prayer Book*, pages 188–189, Chapter II, verse 9–14.

The Great March. "The School That Saved a People"—pages 52–61. "The Temple in Ruins"—pages 65–68.

Great Men in Israel. "A School That Saved a Nation"—pages 27–30.

Great Jews since Bible Times. "The Burning Torch"—pages 24–27.

SOMETHING TO THINK ABOUT

1. People often say that Yohanan's school at Yabneh saved the Jewish people. Is that true? How?
2. At one time Kohanim and Levites were the chief leaders and servants of the Jewish people. Now Rabbis and teachers have taken their place. What brought this change about?

Why Did the Jewish People Revolt Again?

WITHIN a period of fifty years after the dreadful Tisha b'Ab when the Romans destroyed Jerusalem and burnt the Temple, the Jewish people was again living calmly and peacefully. Those who had been captured and sold as slaves had either been bought back and freed by fellow Jews or had died. The poor families were helped to regain some of their lost possessions. Those who were brought or came of their own free will to Europe, Africa, and distant parts of Asia, built synagogues and schools, and continued to live as loyal Jews. The rabbis and teachers who came from the schools in Palestine taught them how to observe their religion. When they were in doubt as to what a law meant or how a custom was to be observed, they turned to the Sanhedrin in Yabneh for information. Slowly, sorrow, pain, and trouble were forgotten.

1. WHY DID JEWS AGAIN PLAN TO REVOLT?

In Palestine, the Jews living in the cities organized themselves and chose leaders to govern them. They appointed judges for the courts, teachers for the schools, caretakers for the synagogues, and inspectors of weights and measures for the market places. The leaders of each city possessed much power. They compelled parents to send their sons to school, made sure that business men used honest weights and measures, and fined any one who disobeyed their rules. The people were thus strongly united.

Learning was especially desired by all observant Jews. For all realized that one had to be learned in the law, if he wished to be a real Jew. An unlearned person was considered an unworthy Jew, and was looked down upon. They called him an "Am Ha-arez" —a man of the land—one who did not even know the religious customs of his own people.

Does it not seem strange to you that the people who loved peace, lived peacefully, and admired learning so much that others later called them "The People of the Book," should have again risen in revolt against mighty Rome which had crushed their armies so completely? And yet that is exactly what the Jews did. Let us see what happened.

The revolt did not begin in Palestine, but in Egypt. Less than fifty years after the war in Palestine, a Roman Emperor decided to take possession of the countries east of Palestine, including Babylonia, and add them to the Roman Empire. He sent most of his army there to do so. The Jews of Egypt and the nearby lands then saw an opportunity to free themselves from Rome, and rose in revolt. Many men lost their lives, and much money was spent, but in vain. The Romans conquered them. When this bloody war came to an end, the Jews living in Babylonia and the lands nearby revolted and more blood was shed before they, too, were overcome. The Roman Emperor was furious. The Jews were always rising up against him. What was to be done? He decided to break their spirit. He ordered that Jerusalem be rebuilt as a Roman city and that the hill on which the Temple once stood should be used as a place of Roman idol worship. This decision enraged the Jews in Palestine.

Other rulings of the emperor angered the people even more. They felt that the Romans were trying to make them miserable. But what were they to do?

Answer the questions to Topic I of Chapter 14.

II. WHAT KIND OF LEADER STIRRED THE PEOPLE?

A great scholar, called Akiba, advised the Jews to revolt. Who was Akiba? What led him to urge the Jews on to another bloody war?

In his youth, Akiba had been an ignorant shepherd lad. He knew little of religion, and even less of government. He was in fact an Am Ha-arez. But, fortunately, he won the love of a maiden who knew the value of learning. She was the daughter of a rich merchant, who lived very comfortably and met many scholars who visited her home. Before marrying Akiba, she made him promise that he would devote himself to study. When her father discovered that her husband was an Am Ha-arez, he became so angry that he drove her from his home. But the young woman had courage. She went to live by herself in a miserable hut and sent Akiba off to another city to carry on his studies.

When the shepherd first came to school, he almost lost courage; he could not understand what was being taught. A kindly teacher led him outside and showed him a big rock with many holes in it. He pointed to the rock and said:

"Soft rain water made these holes in the hard rock by beating on it day after day, and year after year. Anyone will succeed who works continuously. You, too, will succeed if you study unceasingly. Just study, study, study! Then you will know everything that you want to learn! Then you will succeed!"

Thus encouraged, Akiba gave himself up to the study of the Torah. Day and night he studied. He ate little, and slept little, but studied much. He used every waking minute for studying the Torah. Before long, Akiba's teachers realized that he was an excellent student, and they encouraged him to learn more and more. After a number of years he became a teacher. Akiba was an Am Ha-arez no longer.

A legend tells that Akiba returned to his home town after an absence of twelve years. Before entering the house, Akiba heard his poor, overworked wife tell one of her neighbors that she was so proud of her husband's learning and so eager to have him become a truly great scholar that she was even ready to let him carry on his studies for another twelve years. Akiba turned back, without entering the house, and returned to his studying and teaching.

At the end of twenty-four years, he finally came

back to his home town, the most famous rabbi in Palestine, known to all as "Tanna." His father-in-law, not knowing who the Tanna really was, asked him: "May I help my daughter who angered me by marrying an Am Ha-arez?"

Akiba said: "If the Am Ha-arez became learned, would you still be angry?"

"If he only knew how to recite a prayer, I would be happy."

Akiba then replied: "I am your daughter's husband."

His father-in-law was so happy that he gave most of his fortune to Akiba.

The Tanna soon opened a college for the study of the Oral and Written Law. Many pupils came to him, and it is said that during his lifetime, he taught almost twenty-five thousand students. To help his scholars, Akiba collected and arranged much of the Oral Law which had grown up since the days of Ezra. This was a necessary task because so many new laws had been passed by the Tannaim, since the days of Yohanan ben Zakkai. Rabbi Akiba did not write out the laws in a book because it was considered wrong to write down the Oral Law. He did, however, make notes of them for his own use. Some of these, we still have in the Talmud.

Now Rabbi Akiba loved his people and suffered deeply whenever they were hurt. When he learned what had happened to the Jews in Egypt and Babylonia, he was grieved. But when he heard of the decision to build a Roman city where Jerusalem had been, to erect a temple to an idol on the holy hill where the Temple of God had stood, and to forbid Jews to practice some of their ancient customs, he felt that the Romans were insulting God Himself. But what could he do? The Tanna was no fighter. He could handle a book but not a sword. He could give advice on the Law, but he knew nothing of war.

Answer the questions to Topic II.

III. WHAT WAS THE RESULT OF THE TROUBLE BETWEEN ROME AND THE JEWS?

But in the year 135, which is almost 1800 years ago, a warrior appeared. Bar-Kokheba (son of a star) was his name. Bar-Kokheba was strong, fearless, and a good leader of men. To the rabbi he seemed to be a second Judah Maccabee. Through Bar-Kokheba, Akiba hoped to free the Jews from the cruel Romans. And so the scholar Akiba advised his students and friends to join the fighter Bar-Kokheba.

The call of the Tanna was heard throughout the land. Farmers left their fields, laborers their tools, business men their stores, and students their books. All went to join the army of Bar-Kokheba and help drive the Romans out of the land.

With an army of over 100,000, Bar-Kokheba attacked the Romans and drove them out of Palestine. Hopes ran high. The Jews believed that Palestine would soon be free again, as in the days of the Hasmoneans. But it was not to be. Two years after Bar-Kokheba's great victories, the Romans placed at the

A fox was walking along the edge of the river and saw some small fish jumping about in the water in great fear.

head of their army their ablest generals who finally defeated him and destroyed his army.

Once the revolt was over, the Roman emperor decided to make it impossible for Jews ever to rebel again. Knowing that the Torah and the Oral Law kept the Jewish people alive, he determined to make the Jews give them up. Laws were passed forbidding Jews to keep the Sabbath, or to teach the Torah or even study it. Anyone caught disobeying these laws was to be put to death. Of course, very few Jews obeyed these laws and certainly no Tanna did. Rabbi Akiba, the greatest Jewish scholar of his time, did not even take notice of this law, and, like many of his fellow scholars, continued to teach the Torah to all who wished to study it. He was not frightened when he saw his friends arrested by the Romans and put to death. One was burnt alive with the Torah scrolls wrapped about him; another was slain by Roman spears, and a third died by torture. Reports of the sufferings of other teachers and warnings that his own life was in danger, came to him often. But Akiba went on teaching.

One man asked: "Why do you insist on teaching the Torah when it means sacrificing your life?"

Akiba replied: "A fox was walking along the edge of the river and saw some small fish jumping about in the water in great fear. The fox asked the fish: 'What are you afraid of?'

"They replied: 'There is a large fish nearby trying to swallow us. We are trying hard to keep out of its way.'

"The fox then said: 'Why don't you come up on

dry land where you will be safe from the big fish?' But the little fish were clever.

'If we cannot live safely in the water, how can we possibly live on dry land?' "

Akiba then explained his story.

"We Jews are like the fish in the water. We are trying hard to escape from the Romans. The Torah to us is like water to the fish. They cannot live without water, and we cannot live without the Torah; we must therefore continue to study it, even if some of us will be caught and destroyed by Rome."

The Romans found him one day, busy as usual, in the study and the teaching of the Torah. They threw him into prison and sentenced him to death by torture. Dying, Rabbi Akiba repeated this prayer, which we still recite each day:

"Shema Yisrael, Adonoy Elohenu, Adonoy Ehod! —Hear O Israel! The Lord our God, the Lord is One!"

Thus Akiba died, but the Jewish people lived on.

The people did not forget the men who gave up their lives for the study of the Torah and who fought for freedom from Rome. Many stories are still told about them.

One story says that Bar-Kokheba was so strong that he could catch the big stones thrown at him by the Roman machines, and throw them back at his enemies. Another tells that he could tear up a tree by its roots while riding past it on horseback.

Other stories explain why we celebrate Lag Be-Omer.

Lag Be-Omer got its name from an ancient Jewish custom. On the second day of Passover, the farmers brought to the Temple an offering of a measure of barley. The measure was called Omer. Exactly fifty days later they brought their first ripe fruits to the Temple and celebrated Shabuot. To be sure of the date of Shabuot, they counted fifty days after bringing the Omer of barley. The thirty-third day of the count is called Lag Be-Omer because *Lag* is composed of two letters Lamed—representing the number 30 and Gimmel standing for 3.

One story about Lag Be-Omer tells that a plague once broke out among Akiba's pupils. Hundreds of them died of the dreadful disease. About two weeks before Shabuot, the day of Lag Be-Omer, it came to an end, to the joy of all Jews. And so the thirty-third day or Lag Be-Omer marked the celebration.

Another story tells that a certain rabbi fled to a cave to escape the Romans. On Lag Be-Omer his scholars came to him for their instruction. They enjoyed their lesson so much that it was like a holiday to them and so school children still look upon it as *their* holiday, on which they take hikes into the woods, engage in athletic contests, and play with bows and arrows.

Lag Be-Omer is a joyous occasion and yet it is filled with the sad memories of the Tanna Akiba and the warrior Bar-Kokheba. We call it a scholar's festival in honor of men like Akiba who gave up their lives so that the knowledge of the Torah might continue among Jews. Nowadays, we use the week of Lag Be-

Omer for becoming acquainted with new Jewish books and buying them for our homes and Temple libraries. Do so this year!

Answer the questions to Topic III.

ADDITIONAL READING

The Great March. Stories about Rabbi Akiba are very great in number. There are three in this book; the first story, "The Shepherd Rabbi" begins on page 80, the second story, "The Cock, The Donkey, and The Candle," begins on page 88, and the third story "Fish out of Water" on page 94. You will no doubt enjoy reading all the three stories.

Great Men in Israel. Read "When Giants Roamed Palestine" on pages 34-36, and "The Old Man of Bethar"—pages 37-39.

Great Jews since Bible Times. Read "Akiba the Peaceful Soldier"—pages 28-31, and "Bar-Kokhba the Son of a Star"—pages 32-35.

SOMETHING TO THINK ABOUT

1. Should we now celebrate Lag Be-Omer? How?
2. Did the Tanna Akiba help or hurt his fellow-Jews? Why do you think so?
3. The leaders of the United States government want us to be good Americans. Yet they *encourage* us Jews to study the Torah and to live according to its laws. Why did the Roman emperors who wanted to make good Romans out of the Jews, make every effort to *prevent* them from learning the Torah?

What Was the Last Achievement in Palestine?

AKIBA and many of his friends died, so that Judaism might live. Their example encouraged others to disregard the Roman laws, and to continue to study the Torah and follow its commandments. Many died; but others fled to neighboring countries, especially Babylonia, which did not belong to Rome. In one way or another, they managed to live in accordance with the laws of God, until a new emperor withdrew the Roman laws forbidding the Jews to observe their religion.

1. WHY WAS IT NECESSARY TO ARRANGE THE ORAL LAW?

The Tannaim then scattered throughout the land, and opened schools for the study of the Torah, in whatever city or town they happened to settle. Each one taught the Law in his own way and explained it in the manner which seemed most reasonable to him. Several differing explanations were possible, as most of the laws of the Bible had not been given a definite form by the Anshe Keneset Ha-gedolah or the Sanhedrin. The opinions of the rabbis remained unwritten, to show that the Oral Law was less holy than the

Bible, and might be changed when necessary. A few scholars, like the Tanna Akiba, *did* make notes, but they kept them on secret scrolls for personal use only.

As the years went by, the number of oral laws kept increasing. Each Tanna added his opinions to those of the teachers who came before him. It became more and more difficult to know the laws and to understand them because:

1. There were so many that even scholars could not remember all of them.

2. Tannaim sometimes disagreed among themselves as to the correct meaning of some of the laws. But they knew that there were enough learned men ready to explain any problem that might come up; and that if, in spite of that, some unimportant laws *were* overlooked, that would not be a serious matter.

But some of the Tannaim were worried. They had reason enough! Most of the people had to depend on the few learned men, to explain the law. The Oral Law had grown so large and had become so difficult, that only a few scholars knew it well. These scholars could do their work, as long as the colleges for the study of the Jewish law were open. But what would happen if they were closed? How could they teach the people, then? And they feared that the schools might, at any time, be closed. A cruel emperor might order it, just as the Roman emperor had done in the time of Akiba; or, possibly, the people themselves might become too poor to pay for the upkeep of the schools. Should such a calamity occur, the entire Oral

. . . scattered throughout the land.

Law might be forgotten. How real these fears were, you will learn in the coming chapters.

Answer the questions to Topic I of Chapter 15.

II. HOW DID JUDAH HA-NASI SOLVE THE PROBLEM?

To make sure that the Oral Law would be remembered and obeyed, the Tannaim decided to put it into a form that would be easy to learn and to remember. The person who did most of the actual work of arranging it, was the learned Judah Ha-Nasi, the last of the great Tannaim. (Nasi is a title, meaning President. Judah was known as Ha-Nasi because he was President of the Sanhedrin.) The Tanna was so learned that people called him "the Rabbi." Whenever "the Rabbi" was mentioned, every one knew who was meant, just as we know who is meant when one says "the President." It is said that Judah was born on the very day that Akiba died, and was gifted with an equally strong love of learning and an equally great faith in God.

The Tanna Judah Ha-Nasi was well suited for the task of collecting the Oral Law and setting it in proper order. He was, first of all, the most learned man of his time. When a lad, Judah had studied Torah with his father. Later he entered a college. In a little while, he had learned all he could from the teacher in charge, and had gone to another college. From there, he went to a third school. So he continued for many years, attending school after school, learning the wisdom of each Tanna. By the time he grew up, Judah knew more than any of his teachers, and became the principal of a college for the study of the Torah and the Oral Law. He taught so well, that he learned even more by teaching than by studying. He himself said: "I learned much from my teachers, more from my associates, and most of all from my pupils." No wonder people often spoke of him as "the Rabbi."

Judah was more than just a learned man. He was also most highly respected by the people, so that his word was as good as law. He was a descendant of the gentle scholar, Hillel, of whom you read in an earlier chapter. Judah's forefathers had stood at the head of the Sanhedrin for generations before him, and Judah himself became Nasi of the Sanhedrin when his father died.

As Nasi, Judah alone had the right to decide who could be a rabbi. He alone appointed the rabbis to the different communities in Palestine, and even outside. He selected the judges for the courts, and it was he who collected the taxes for the Roman governors. His power was such that he might well have been called, "King of the Jews."

Judah was fortunate also in that he inherited great wealth. Unlike many other Tannaim who worked as shoemakers, smiths, or at some other trade, Judah was in a position to give all his time to study and to his duties as Nasi of the Sanhedrin. He had enough, not only for his own family, but also for the poor students who attended the colleges. When a great famine visited Palestine, he distributed food among his scholars, and among all the poor of the land. This shows us that

Judah was not merely a prince who liked to give orders, but a true friend of the people. Judah was a Nasi who deserved that title.

From his travels about the country, Judah knew that the Oral Law was difficult to follow. From his talks with Roman officials, he realized that some day the Palestinian schools might be forced to close their doors even if the people did not become too poor to support them.

Judah, therefore, determined to arrange the Oral Law in a definite form which would be easy to remember.

Answer the questions to Topic II.

III. WHAT IS THE MISHNAH?

The Rabbi first collected all the secret scrolls prepared by the Tannaim for their own use. He also collected all the sayings of the Tannaim, the comments of the Anshe Keneset Ha-gedolah, and the decisions of the Sanhedrin. All these sayings, laws, and explanations of laws and customs he arranged, with the help of his students, into six divisions. When he put together all the laws dealing with the same subject, he sometimes found two or more different opinions on how a certain law was to be carried out. Judah chose the one he considered correct and recommended that *it only* should be followed. When he discovered that certain laws were not clearly stated, he worded them so that all should be able to understand. Laws that needed further explanations were also made clear. He simplified the collection further by using pure Hebrew even though most of the other Tannaim spoke a mixture of Hebrew and Aramaic. When the task was done, about 1700 years ago, Judah named his collection of the Oral Laws, Mishnah (meaning, study). A few of its most interesting chapters you may read in your Siddur, under the heading, "Sayings of the Fathers" or "Ethics of the Fathers."

Let us learn a little more about the Mishnah. The book is divided into six parts.

The first is called "Seeds," and contains all laws and customs which a farmer in Palestine had to know. For example, he had to give a tenth of his crop to the Kohanim and Levites; he had to leave a small part of his field uncut so that poor people could take it; if he forgot to take some grain away, it was to be left for the poor; if some grain was dropped in the harvesting, it, too, was to remain for those who had no other way of getting food. He was not allowed to plow the ground during the seventh, or "Sabbatical" year. Anything that grew in the field during that year, belonged to anyone who wished to take it.

The second part of the Mishnah is called "Festivals" and gives all the laws that we must know in order to observe our holy-days such as the Sabbath, Passover, Shabuot, Sukkot, Rosh Hashanah, and fast days such as Yom Kippur and Tisha b'Ab. Thus on Sukkot, we are commanded to eat in a "Sukkah" with a roof made of leaves and branches; on Passover, we must eat Mazzot, and use special holiday dishes; on Yom Kippur

. . . a "Sukkah" with a roof made of leaves and branches; . . .

we may neither work nor eat but we are to stay in the synagogue and pray.

The third part is called "Women," and deals with laws on marriage and divorce.

The fourth division is called "Damages." It tells us how to deal with people who cause damage to others, by taking or breaking things that do not belong to them. It also tells what laws we obey when we have or wish to get property. Incidentally, it may interest you to know that this part of the Mishnah includes the "Sayings of the Fathers," parts of which you were advised to read.

The fifth part is called "Holy Things," and contains special rules for Kohanim and Levites.

The last part, "Purification," tells us how to keep ourselves pure and clean.

The six parts of the Mishnah contain the Oral Law as it was known in the time of Judah Ha-Nasi.

Answer the questions to Topic III.

IV. HOW DID OUR PEOPLE LEARN THE MISHNAH?

After completing the Mishnah, Judah did not allow scribes to make copies of it. He still felt that the Oral Law should not be written down. To make his Mishnah known, he had a number of his pupils memorize it word for word. When called upon, these men repeated any part of the Mishnah that was wanted, and they remembered every word of it so well, that few errors were ever found in their repetition. These men served in the colleges in place of books.

So excellent was this Mishnah, that the scholars living after Judah, studied it as carefully as the Tannaim had studied the Torah. The discussions and decisions of these later rabbis, called Amoraim, are found in the "Gemara" which took another three hundred years to finish.

Since those days down to our own times, Jewish scholars continued to study and explain the Mishnah and Gemara, together known as the Talmud. In fact, until only fifty years ago, many Jews who lived in the East-European countries, including Russia, Poland, Lithuania, Austria, Roumania, and others, knew the Talmud better than the Torah. It was the Talmud over which they spent days and nights in study; and only rarely did they turn the leaves of the Bible.

Judah Ha-Nasi accomplished a fine piece of work when he made up the Mishnah, and we are still grateful to him for his valuable services. The Mishnah was the last great achievement in Palestine. In the years following, no Palestinian scholars arose, equal to Judah, Akiba, or Yohanan ben Zakkai. Most of the schools were gradually forced to close, and the majority of the people sadly left the land. Palestine became a country with a glorious past but a gloomy present. It is interesting to note that despite the great poverty of the land, men continued to study the "Law." A Palestinian Talmud (called Talmud Yerushalmi or the Jerusalem Talmud) was compiled, the merit of which is still considered great.

Answer the questions to Topic IV.

ADDITIONAL READING

Prayerbook. At the beginning of Chapter II of the "Sayings of the Fathers," you will find some words of wisdom spoken by Judah Ha-Nasi. In the *Union Prayerbook* you will find them on page 152. In the *Authorized Daily Prayer Book* see pages 186–187, Chapter II, verse 1.

The Great March. Some of the Tannaim about whom we have been unable to study in class also were interesting people. Would you like to read about them? Try "The Guardians of the Torah," beginning on page 99; "Ki-Tov—'Twas Good" on page 105; "ABC at Twenty-Two," page 69; and "The Wicked Neighbor," page 76.

Great Jews since Bible Times. Read "The Rabbi and the Emperor," beginning on page 36.

SOMETHING TO THINK ABOUT

1. When you read the contents of the Mishnah, you must have felt that the Jews then had a great number of laws to obey. Do we have as many now as our fathers had then? (Before answering, think of the number of lawyers we now have and the great, thick volumes they are always busy reading.)
2. Is it worth our while to learn the Mishnah? Why?
3. Would you call Judah Ha-Nasi a great man? Why?

How Did Babylonia Become the Center of Jewish Learning?

JUDAH had been very wise in his decision to put the Oral Law in a form easy to learn. When he died, some 1700 years ago, there were no great scholars to follow him. Several of his best students left Palestine. Those who remained were not equal to him or to the other great Tannaim—Yohanan ben Zakkai or Akiba. The new teachers could neither attract many students, nor teach them much. Besides, the people had little time or energy for study. They had to work so hard to pay the heavy taxes demanded by the Romans, that they were scarcely able to earn enough for food. And so many of the schools had to close their doors.

The Oral Law, however, was not forgotten. Judah had arranged the Mishnah so that it could be easily learned and understood. The Nasi who followed took care to have the people live in accordance with its commands.

1. WHY THE JEWS WENT FROM PALESTINE TO BABYLONIA

The Jews in Palestine no longer made up the most important Jewish community. The greatest scholars, as well as the Temple, were gone. The last great achievement of the Jews in Palestine was Judah's Mishnah. Many Palestinian Jews continued to study. A number of their scholars produced a fine explanation of the laws in the Mishnah, called "Gemara." But the Palestinian schools were no longer as good as those in other countries, and Palestinian Jews were no longer as learned as their brethren living in other lands. More and more Jews left Palestine until finally it became only a reminder of a glorious past. Until recent times, a mere handful of Jews dwelt in the land.

But Judaism did not die out with the schools in Palestine. New houses of learning were built in another land, in Babylonia, the land into which Jews were exiled when their first Temple was destroyed, and out of which came Ezra the Sofer (the Scribe).

From your previous study, you no doubt recall that Babylonia lay between the Tigris and Euphrates rivers. It was well watered. Many canals brought the life-giving waters of the Tigris and Euphrates to the farms and vineyards. Farmers prospered. Land was cheap and could be had from the government by the payment of a small tax. And so, many Jews became farmers. Others earned their living by taking care of the canals. In the cities, Jews worked as bakers, weavers, tailors, wood cutters, iron workers, and ship builders, or became merchants. Babylonia was a country where no healthy, honest man had to depend on charity.

The rulers of the land were Persians, the fiercest enemies of Rome. To carry on their wars successfully, they wanted the help of the Jewish people and, there-

Farmers prospered.

fore, treated them well. To win their favor, the kings allowed the Jews to govern themselves almost as if they were in their own country.

Answer the questions to Topic I of Chapter 16.

II. HOW WERE THE BABYLONIAN JEWS GOVERNED?

At the head of the Babylonian Jews stood a prince who was a descendant of the house of David. His official title was "Resh-Galuta," which means "Head of the Exiles." The Resh Galuta was expected to keep the Jews peaceful and happy. For this purpose, the Resh Galuta was given great powers over his people. One who committed a crime, was arrested by the officers of the Resh Galuta, and brought up for trial before a judge whom the Resh Galuta had appointed. If found guilty, he was punished by a fine, a beating, or imprisonment. The Resh Galuta also selected men to visit the places where Jewish merchants carried on their business and examine the weights and measures. A merchant who used false scales was promptly arrested, placed on trial, and punished if found guilty.

The Jews of Babylonia were well satisfied with their own government, and highly honored its head, the Resh Galuta. In the synagogue, the Resh Galuta occupied a seat at the front. When called upon to read a selection from the Bible during the services, he did not have to come up to the pulpit like the other people; the Sefer Torah was brought to his seat. Outside the synagogue, people bowed before him and made way for him when, surrounded by many servants, he passed by, wearing his beautiful silk cloak fastened with a golden girdle. In his home, the most learned and respected Jews used to gather. Occasionally, he visited the king and was received with great honor.

The Babylonian Jews were happy. It was easy for them to earn a living and to follow the commandments of the Torah. Their own Resh Galuta ruled over them, and no one had the power to force them to disobey the laws of God as the Romans had tried to force their brethren in Palestine.

Answer the questions to Topic II.

III. WHY DID RAB OPEN A SCHOOL IN SURA?

Some of the Babylonian scholars were troubled because most people knew so little of the Torah and still less of the Oral Law. There was not one good school among the few in Babylonia. In former years, a man who wished to be a scholar, had gone to Palestine to study; Hillel and many others did so, but most of the people found it too hard to leave their homes and go so far away. But a fine scholar, known as Rab, finally succeeded in founding a school worthy of the Babylonian Jews. He was one of the men who had gone to Palestine and studied under Judah Ha-Nasi. Being a very capable student, he had learned the Mishnah well and understood it thoroughly. After the death of Judah he returned to Babylonia and was soon appointed by the Resh Galuta as inspector of weights and measures. Rab traveled from city to city, visiting the Jewish business men, and, at the same time, observing their manner of living. He found that the Jews often disobeyed important laws without knowing that they were doing so. Rab then realized how necessary it was to teach Torah and Mishnah and decided to open a school for his brethren in Babylonia. This was not as difficult as it might sound. All he needed was a building in which his pupils could assemble, and benches upon which they might sit. He needed no textbooks, for he knew the Torah and the Mishnah by heart, and expected his pupils to remember what he taught them. Nor did Rab need teachers, principals, or clerks, for he was the whole teaching staff. Rab, therefore, gave up his position as examiner of weights and measures, and opened a college in the city of Sura, because the Jews of that city were least learned and in greatest need of instruction in the Torah.

Answer the questions to Topic III.

IV. HOW DID RAB TEACH?

Students immediately came to Rab's school, eager to learn the Oral Law which had grown up in Palestine. In a short time, he became the most famous scholar in Babylonia, and his school grew tremendously. To teach those who had to work during the daytime, Rab set the hours of instruction for the early morning and evening. So many new students now attended his college that Rab had to choose assistants to help him in his work.

The chief subject taught was the Mishnah, which the Palestinian Tannaim had prepared. This is how they studied. Rab, or one of his assistants, began the lesson by reciting one of the laws of the Mishnah. The students and teachers then discussed its meaning and explained how to carry it out in Babylonia. These discussions were usually quite interesting. The students and teachers often told good stories to make their ideas clear. Some of them were curious fables, but most of the stories dealt with Jewish heroes of long ago. They told of prophets, kohanim, kings, soferim, scholars, and rabbis. Some of these stories, especially about Hillel, Yohanan, and Akiba you know already; others you will be able to read at the end of this lesson, or some other time. The stories helped to lighten the long hours of study and made Rab's college in Sura even more famous.

In addition to teaching in the college, Rab did two other things to spread the knowledge of the "Law" among the Babylonian Jews.

1. He lectured in the synagogue each Sabbath, in the same way as our rabbis do nowadays.

2. He arranged special lectures, twice each year during the two months when men who worked on the farms had some spare time. The one was at the end of the summer, and the other in the middle of the winter. To these special courses, called "Kallas," such great crowds came from the cities and country places round about Sura, that there was not enough room in the city to house them all, and hundreds had to live in tents on the outskirts of the city.

Answer the questions to Topic IV.

He lectured in the synagogue each Sabbath, . . .

V. HOW DID BABYLONIA BECOME THE CENTER OF JEWISH LEARNING?

Rab's college proved to be so successful that the Jews in other cities in Babylonia decided to follow his example. Thus smaller schools were opened in practically every Jewish city in Babylonia. The most famous of these was in Pumbedita. It was second only to the college in Sura. To this school as to the one in Sura, pupils came to study and discuss the Mishnah. Knowledge of the Oral Law thus spread in Babylonia, which now became the center of Jewish learning.

When Rab died, his work was carried on by his Babylonian students. For hundreds of years after, pupils continued to study in Sura, Pumbedita, and other colleges. No longer did Babylonians have to go to Palestine for an education. Their own colleges were, thanks to Rab, the best in the world. Palestinian scholars now came to Babylonia to acquire a thorough knowledge of the Law.

The great rabbis and teachers were now honored with a new title, "Amora," lecturer. The "Tannaim" (teachers) were no more. The Amoraim took their place. No longer was the Torah the chief subject of study. The Mishnah had taken its place. Of course the Torah was respected then as much as it ever had been; but, to carry out the biblical commandments, one had to study the Oral Law found in the Mishnah. Amoraim therefore, generation after generation, continued to study, discuss, and argue about the correct meaning of the Mishnah. For three hundred years this study went on. All of the discussions were carried on in a mixture of Aramaic and Hebrew—the language spoken by the Jews of Babylonia. At the end of that time, Amoraim collected and arranged these explanations of the Mishnah into a new set of books called the "Gemara." We shall learn more about the Gemara later.

The credit for making Babylonia the center of Jewish learning belongs largely to the first great Amora, Rab. He will always be remembered as the man who brought the knowledge of the Oral Law to Babylonia. He was the one who did most to make Babylonia the new center of Jewish learning.

Answer the questions to Topic V.

ADDITIONAL READING

The Great March. Some of the curious stories told by the rabbis during their discussions are retold in this book. Read "The Cock, the Donkey, and the Candle," on pages 88–93.

Great Men in Israel. A legend about Rab is told in the story "School Days in Babylon," on page 43.

SOMETHING TO THINK ABOUT

1. What is a "Center of Learning?" Do you know what cities may be called "Centers of Jewish Learning in America?" Why?
2. Was the study of the Oral Law more important in Babylonia in the days of Rab than it is in America today? Why?

How Was the Talmud Made?

Did you ever hear of a set of books that took a thousand years to finish? No? Well, there is a set like that. Hundreds of scholars worked on it, generation after generation. The beginnings were made in Palestine in the days of Ezra the Sofer, and Nehemiah the governor, some 2400 years ago. The work was finished in Babylonia by the last of the great Amoraim, about 1400 years ago. A single set of books that took so many scholars so many years to complete must indeed be worth knowing. Would you like to learn about it?

1. THE NECESSITY OF REARRANGING THE ORAL LAW

Perhaps without knowing it, you have already learned something about this piece of literature. You recall that, in the days of Ezra and Nehemiah, scholars began a careful study of the Bible. Many laws never known before, or perhaps old customs which had been forgotten, became known, as a result of their labors. More scholars, judges, and especially Tannaim, issued additional laws over a period of several hundred years. Finally all the explanations, comments, decisions, and additions making up the Oral Law, so called because it was never written out, were collected and arranged by Judah Ha-Nasi, 1700 years ago. Judah's Mishnah, completed fully 700 years after Ezra had begun to develop the Oral Law, contains all the important laws that had grown up after the Bible was given its present form. But the Mishnah is only a small part of the set of books we are discussing, though it is a most important one. As you have learned already, the Amoraim, both in Palestine and Babylonia, kept discussing, explaining, and adding to the Oral Law of the Mishnah for another three hundred years. In the year 500, which is slightly more than 1400 years ago, the completed Oral Law was collected, arranged, and written out in full. It was named "Talmud" (study). This magnificent collection we shall now discuss in a little greater detail.

After the Mishnah had been completed in Palestine, the Amora Rab and several of his friends succeeded in building up fine colleges in Babylonia for the further study of the Oral Law. Year after year, and generation after generation, this study went on. Gradually, the knowledge of the Oral Law became widespread.

Some of the less important laws were known only to Amoraim of certain colleges, and certain teachings of the rabbis were given different meanings by the Amoraim. And so, *no one Amora* knew and understood the entire Oral Law. Now the Oral Law was not written out. It could be learned only by attending one of the colleges. Since the heads of the schools did not always agree on the correct meaning of some of the laws, it was impossible for any one person to know

The Amora himself hired workmen to rebuild the entire house of learning.

them all unless he could attend all the colleges. The wiser Amoraim were not satisfied to know only a part of the teachings contained in the Oral Law. They feared lest some of them be neglected or altogether forgotten. And there was so much to remember that even people with unusually good memories could hardly hope to know the entire Oral Law.

Answer the questions to Topic I of Chapter 17.

II. WHO WAS THE PRINCIPAL WORKER?

The Amora Ashi, who lived about 1500 years ago, decided to arrange the Talmud, just as Judah Ha-Nasi had arranged the Mishnah, 200 years before him. Like Judah, Ashi was well-fitted for the task. When he was young, Ashi studied the Oral Law very thoroughly and his fame as a scholar spread through the land. At that time, there were very few students in Sura, because no great scholars taught in that city. Even the school building where the Amora Rab had once taught, was shabby, and seemed ready to fall apart.

When Ashi was only twenty years old, he decided to reopen the college in Sura. The Amora himself hired workmen to rebuild the entire house of learning. When it was finished, he invited students to come to Sura. Many who came were very poor, and Ashi supported them out of his own funds. His teaching was so fine and showed so much knowledge of the Oral Law that even the other heads of the Babylonian colleges admitted that Ashi was the greatest scholar of his day. His school grew rapidly in size, and became so famous for its learning, that Jews in other lands often wrote asking him about the meaning of certain difficult parts of the Oral Law; and they always accepted his explanations.

Answer the questions to Topic II.

III. HOW DID RABBI ASHI FORM THE TALMUD?

Ashi now undertook to arrange the Talmud. He collected all the discussions that explained a law of the Mishnah and put them together. Some of the discussions which he did not consider worth remembering, he omitted from his collection. Others were not sufficiently clear nor complete; to them he added his own explanations. He included not only the arguments for and against the law, but also the stories and sayings of the Tannaim and Amoraim and comments on the lives and activities of the great teachers.

Ashi did not change Judah's arrangement of the laws found in the Mishnah. Like Judah, Ashi divided his work into six parts. He used for each part the name which Judah had given it. The first part of Rabbi Ashi's collection opens with the words of the first law found in the Mishnah. The Mishnaic Law is followed by all the arguments, stories, and sayings concerning it. After completing the discussion on a certain part of the Mishnah, Ashi quotes the second law and gives all the discussions about it. Thus, the completed work is composed of all the laws of the Mishnah, each followed by the discussions, arguments, explanations, stories, and sayings of the Amoraim.

This second part was called "Gemara." The Mishnah and Gemara combined, form the Talmud.

Now, although Ashi was the most learned Jew of his time, he did not assume that he knew everything and that his work was perfect. He wanted the help and advice of the learned men of his day. And so this is what he did. He followed the example of the great Amoraim, and held Kallas twice each year.

At every Kalla, to which many scholars came, Ashi read aloud the part of the Talmud which he had prepared during the preceding half year. Then the rabbis and pupils present corrected whatever errors he had made and advised him how to improve his work. This he did for many years. When he had finally finished the Talmud, Ashi was not satisfied with his work, and decided to do it all over again. He worked on the Talmud for the rest of his life. When he died, after more than *fifty years* of continuous labor, Ashi had not yet completed the Talmud! His students, however, took up the task. They worked for *fifty years* more, to complete it. Just think! It took almost a hundred years just to collect and arrange the Talmud! But the Talmud was not yet written out completely. It was still kept on secret scrolls and in the minds of a few men who had exceptionally fine memories.

Answer the questions to Topic III.

IV. WHY WAS THE TALMUD FINALLY WRITTEN DOWN?

Before long, however, the Talmud *was* written out in full. There was a good reason for it. The Jews of

Babylonia were beginning to feel the enmity of the Persian rulers. The Persians were worshippers of fire, who wanted all the people, including the Jews, to worship in the same manner. When the kindling of fires on Friday nights was forbidden, the Jews were forced to light their Sabbath candles secretly. That is how it became the custom for Jewish mothers to hide the candle flames from sight by covering their eyes when they recited the blessing over the lights.

Some rulers found other reasons for being unfriendly to the Jews. One Amora who held large Kallas was accused of decreasing the amount of taxes collected from Jews. The officials said that those who came to the Kallas did not pay their taxes to the government. For this reason, the officials wanted to arrest the Amora. He fled, was lost in the forest and died of starvation. At another time, the Jews were forbidden to recite the Shema, or keep the Sabbath. Of course, most Jews disobeyed the laws openly or secretly. Some were arrested and punished; the Resh Galuta himself was put to death; but the people remained loyal to their religion.

Rabbis began to fear that their schools would have to close and that the Talmud might be completely forgotten. They, therefore, took the only sensible step possible to prevent such a calamity. They ordered that the Talmud be written out. Men skilled in writing set to work at once, and for the first time, they wrote out the Talmud in full. They were careful to use every bit of the expensive parchment, and left no spaces at

Jewish mothers hide the candle flames from sight by covering their eyes. . . .

the beginning of paragraphs or between chapters. Pictures were not used. Punctuation was unknown at that time, and so the Talmud was one solid mass of writing.

When it was printed a thousand years later, its form was left unchanged; every page was completely filled with print. These printed copies of the Talmud included explanations prepared by some great scholars who lived long after the Talmud had been finished. The explanations were printed in extremely small letters, difficult for most people to read. Yet, in spite of the fact that every page is filled to the very edge with printed words, the Talmud and its explanations fill eighteen large volumes.

Copies of the Talmud, written on scrolls, were distributed throughout Babylonia. Some finally reached the Jews in Europe. The Oral Law was no longer "oral." It could now be read and studied as was the Bible. Ever since its completion, Jews have been studying the Talmud, despite all of its difficulties. Indeed, the difficulties of the Talmud attracted the Jews, and still do.

Answer the questions to Topic IV.

V. WHY DO WE STILL STUDY THE TALMUD?

Late some afternoon, step into an Orthodox synagogue, and you will probably see a group of Jews studying the Talmud. Each one is bent over a large volume, and follows attentively the reading and explanation of the man seated at the head of the table. At times, the reader stops and a general discussion takes place. This goes on until it is time for evening prayers. This study circle meets daily, including the Sabbath, when the meeting lasts somewhat longer.

The men study one book of the Talmud after another until they have finished the entire set. Then they begin all over again. And they find it just as interesting the second time as they did the first. No one truly interested in the Talmud ever tires of it. Some of the men actually study the entire Talmud twice, and even three times!

A glance over the shoulder of one of these men might make you wonder why people like to study this book so much. It is large and clumsy to handle. The page is crowded with print. There is not a picture anywhere—not even a margin at the beginning of each paragraph. The printed words are in two different sizes, and some of them are so small, that it hurts one's eyes to read them. Nor will you find commas, periods, semicolons, or question marks to help you in your reading. A person studying the Talmud must get along without them.

Students of the Talmud have much greater difficulties to overcome than the small print, or the lack of punctuation marks. The language in which the Talmud is written is hard to understand. You know of course that it is not English; but neither is it Hebrew. It is a mixture of much Aramaic with a little Hebrew. It takes a great deal of time and effort to learn this language.

But even after you know the language of the Talmud you still find many parts of it very hard to understand. It often happens that the meaning of a sentence or of a paragraph is not clear, even though you know the meaning of each word. Or you may not be able to see the connection between one sentence and another which follows it.

In reading the English translation of the Bible you may have found many sentences which are hard to understand, but they are not nearly so difficult as those in the Talmud. However, Jewish scholars are not frightened by difficulties. When a lesson is hard to learn, they simply give it more time and effort. Later you will learn about many such scholars.

Another Talmud, much shorter and much simpler was written in Palestine, by those Amoraim who lived there after the death of Judah Ha-Nasi. The Palestinian Talmud is not well-known at present, but the one written in Babylonia is still widely read.

There are many reasons why the Babylonian Talmud is still studied. It contains the "Oral Law," which many Jews still observe. In its pages one may find beautiful stories of great Jews, good advice for young and old, suggestions on how to live, prayers, and blessings. And the student of history can learn how the Jews lived up to the time of the completion of the Talmud.

All the stories, the history, and the sayings of the wise are known by the Hebrew name "Aggada," meaning, legend, while the laws and their explanations are known as "Halakhah" meaning, law.

In order to become a good Talmudist, many a Russian and Polish Jew began to study the Talmud at the age of seven years, and sometimes even sooner, and kept studying it until he became a full grown man. Even then, he continued his Talmudic studies by coming to the synagogue to study whenever he had any free time. The Talmud is certainly a great book! Perhaps, you, too, will study it when you grow older. You will surely find it interesting and worthwhile.

Answer the questions to Topic V.

ADDITIONAL READING

The Prayerbook. In the *Union Prayerbook,* Vol. II (for the High Holy Days) there are three selections from the Talmud given on pages 294–297. If you read them, you will learn what were some of the questions in which the rabbis were interested.

Great Men in Israel. One of the Amoraim who had an important part in the making of the Talmud was Rabbi Huna. Read about him in the story, "Huna, the Generous Farmer," pages 46–48.

Rabbinic Wisdom. Jennie Reizenstein prepared a little book containing a large number of fine stories taken from the Talmud. All of them are worth reading. Borrow the book from the library and read as many of them as you like.

SOMETHING TO THINK ABOUT

1. There are two different kinds of discussion in the Talmud. One is Halakhah while the other is Ag-

gada. Which of the two types interests most of the people who study the Talmud at present? Which kind interested the people 1400 years ago? Why?

2. The Tanna Judah Ha-Nasi arranged the Mishnah while the Amora Ashi did his best to complete the Talmud. Whose task, do you think, was the more difficult? Why?

What Turned the Attention of the Jews to the Bible?

THE past few chapters have described how the Oral Law grew up over a period of a thousand years, and how the Talmud was finally completed and written out. In reading those chapters you must have realized that, despite the importance of the Talmud, the people did not devote all their time to it. With the exception of the scholars, people spent most of their time then as we do now. They worked for a living and spent their leisure much as we do today. Unlike many of us, however, they attended the synagogue more regularly and devoted several hours each day to the study of the Oral Law.

After the Talmud was finally completed, it became the chief subject of study for grown-up men. They considered the Bible too easy to require much attention. Scholars rarely devoted any time to it. But about two hundred years after the Talmud had been completed, the Jews began to realize that the Bible was, after all, as important as the Talmud; perhaps even more important.

Let us learn what again turned the attention of the Jews to the Bible.

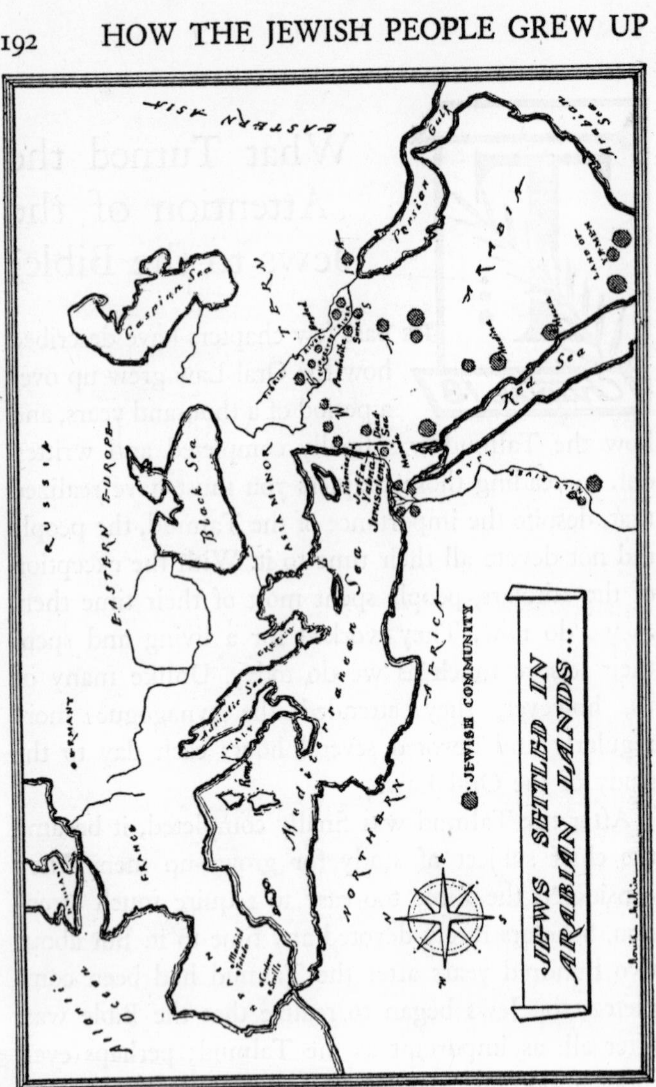
JEWS SETTLED IN ARABIAN LANDS ...
JEWISH COMMUNITY
EASTERN ASIA
Caspian Sea
Black Sea
Persian Gulf
Red Sea
Mediterranean Sea
Adriatic Sea
ASIA MINOR
EASTERN EUROPE
RUSSIA
GERMANY
FRANCE
ITALY
Rome
EGYPT
NORTHERN AFRICA
ARABIA
LAND OF YEMEN
Jaffa
Yabna
Jerusalem
Dead Sea

1. HOW DID JEWS LIVE IN ARABIA?

The story begins in the deserts of Arabia. Jews lived there as well as in Babylonia, though in smaller numbers. They had come to Arabia when the Romans had destroyed Jerusalem and the Temple in the year 70, which was over 1860 years ago. More came in later years. They settled in many different parts of Arabia, particularly in the fertile land of Yemen and in the city now called Medina. Many had even settled in the desert. The Jews and Arabs were friendly toward one another. They believed that they were all descendants of the same ancestor, called Shem. (For this reason Jews and Arabs are called Semites, and their enemies, Anti-Semites.) How friendly Jews and Arabs were, can be learned from the following story.

An Arab left his daughter in the care of a Jew, called Samuel. Enemies of the Arab came to Samuel and demanded that he surrender the girl to them. Samuel refused. Then his own son was captured by that Arab's enemies. They told Samuel that, unless, he gave up the girl, his son would be put to death. But the Jew could not surrender the girl without breaking faith with his friend, the Arab. Rather than do that, Samuel let his son die. Ever since that day, the Arabs compliment people who keep faith by saying they are "as faithful as Samuel."

Because of their true friendship, Jews and Arabs lived happily together. Those in the northern part of Arabia, which was mostly desert land, raised cattle

. . . they paid a good deal of attention to the education of their children.

and sheep for their living, while those in the southern part were farmers. Many Jews were also merchants. They traded not only with each other but also with the people living in the far-off lands of India and Persia.

As we might have expected, they paid a good deal of attention to the education of their children. They taught them Bible and a little of the Oral Law. Unlike the Babylonian Jews, they did not devote as much of their time to Jewish studies. The children also learned the language and the poetry of the Arabs.

Answer the questions to Topic I of Chapter 18.

II. WHAT DID JEWS TEACH THE ARABS?

While the Jews learned Arabic from their neighbors, they in turn, taught the Arabs religion. The Arabs worshipped the sun, moon, stars, and idols. When the more thoughtful ones became acquainted with the Jewish religion, they felt that it was much finer than their own. Many of them then became Jews. Among them were the King of Yemen and many of his followers. Thus a new Jewish kingdom came into being. But, it lasted only a few short years, for the Christian king of a neighboring country attacked Yemen and conquered it.

This misfortune did not prevent the Arabs from learning more about the Jewish religion. As time passed, many more of them became Jewish. For about 500 years, the number of Jewish Arabs kept increasing. Then there came a change. It was about 1300 years ago that an Arab, called Mohammed, developed a new religion. Mohammed was one of those who realized that idol worship was not true religion; but he did not wish to join the Jews or Christians. From his talks with Jews, Mohammed realized that there was only one God, and that He alone should be worshipped. The Jewish method of worship through prayer also appealed to him. In fact, he considered the Jewish religion a good example of what a true religion should be.

After years of thinking, Mohammed developed the religion called after its founder, Mohammedanism. The followers of this religion look upon Mohammed as we Jews do upon Moses. They believe in one invisible God to whom they pray several times a day. Friday is their day of rest, and the Koran (a holy book containing the teachings of Mohammed) is their Bible.

The Mohammedan religion spread quickly among all the Arabs, for two reasons: (1) Mohammed ordered his followers to kill any one who refused to accept the new religion. (2) Arabs living near the Jews learned to dislike idol worship, and were glad to adopt the new religion which taught the belief in one God.

Answer the questions to Topic II.

III. HOW DID JEWS LIVE UNDER ARABIC RULE?

Fired with zeal for their new religion, the Arabs united and set out to conquer the world. At first, the

Mohammedans attacked the Jews for refusing to give up their religion, but they soon realized that this was foolish and made friends with them. The Jews, mistreated both by the Christians and the Persian fire-worshippers, helped the Mohammedans. In a short time Mohammedans conquered all of Persia, Palestine, Egypt, the countries in the northern part of Africa, and finally Spain, in the southwestern corner of Europe.

In return for their help, the Arabs befriended the Jews, wherever they found them. The Jews in Babylonia benefited greatly. All laws against them were withdrawn. The Resh Galuta was again made the Jewish ruler and a high official of the new government.

The colleges now became greater and more important than before; more students came to the schools; many of them were poor. To make it possible for them to carry on their studies, they had to be given a home, food, and clothes. The colleges also needed teachers and parchment and many copies of the Talmud. No one man could now follow the example of Judah Ha-Nasi, or of Ashi, each of whom had supported a college, single-handed. Large sums of money were needed. But the Jews supported the colleges willingly. Some of the money came from Babylonia, but a good deal also came from Jews living in the different parts of Europe, Asia, and Africa.

At the head of each college, was a very learned and much respected scholar known as "Gaon" (Excellency). He had many important duties. He helped raise the money for the college. He appointed the teachers. He answered questions about the meaning of Jewish laws. Many of the questions came from Babylonia, and some from people living in lands far away. The messengers who came with the questions, usually brought some gifts for the college. The Gaon generally read these questions at the Kalla and answered them with the help of the teachers and students present.

The Geonim of Sura and Pumbedita had another important duty—that of appointing the Resh Galuta. They usually chose the eldest son of the former Resh Galuta; but they were not obliged to do so, if they had good reason for choosing another.

Answer the questions to Topic III.

IV. WHAT LED JEWS BACK TO THE BIBLE?

One choice of a Resh Galuta caused great excitement among the Jews. It led many of them away from the Talmud and back to the Bible. About a hundred years after the Arabs had conquered Persia—that is, about 1200 years ago—Mohammedan scholars began to study the Koran. As a result of their studies, they found that many of their oral laws differed from those written in the Koran. They therefore urged their Mohammedan brethren to follow the directions of the Koran rather than those which they had learned orally from their fathers.

Some Jews followed the example of the Arabic

He was thrown into prison.

scholars and began to study the Bible to learn whether the Oral Law of the Talmud, was completely in accordance with the Written Law of the Bible. The leader of these men was Anan ben David, the nephew of the Resh Galuta. His studies of the Bible made him realize its importance and he began to feel that his people should study it instead of the Talmud. His beliefs displeased the Geonim who felt that the study of the Talmud was more important. They therefore refused to appoint him as Resh Galuta when his childless uncle died, but chose his younger brother instead. This enraged Anan, who declared that he was the true Resh Galuta. For this, he was arrested by the Arabian officers and thrown into prison.

A short time later, Anan was set free and permitted to go to Palestine. There, he and his followers began to read the Bible carefully. To make sure that they understood the meaning of the Torah, they studied Hebrew grammar. As a result of their work, they decided that the Oral Law of the Talmud should not be followed. Those Jews who agreed with Anan became known as "Karaites" which means "those who follow the Torah." They are so called because they try to live in accordance with what they find written in the Torah, and pay no attention whatever to the Oral Law of the Talmud.

The Karaites now tried to carry out the laws of the Torah without using the explanations of the Talmud. Instead of the Oral Law they used explanations of their own which do not appear to have been any better than those found in the Talmud. Thus, Karaites do not celebrate the holiday of Hanukkah, because it is not mentioned in the Bible. Purim is observed by two days of sorrow and fasting, because Haman tried to destroy the Jews. The Sabbath is not a day of joy, but only a day of rest. No fire or light is found in their homes on that day. No warm food is eaten, and, if the weather is cold, the Karaites wrap themselves up in blankets and stay in bed the entire Sabbath day. Furthermore, according to their explanation of the Bible, no animal is considered *kosher,* except the deer and the dove.

Naturally the Jews who believed in the Oral Law did not consider the Karaites observant Jews, while the Karaites, in their turn, did not consider the others, good Jews; and so the groups separated. Karaites would not marry Jews who observed the Oral Law nor did they worship in their synagogues. They lived apart from the rest of the Jewish people.

Karaites did help the Jewish people in one way. They made everyone realize how important it was to study the Torah. By writing books on the meaning of the Torah and on Hebrew grammar, the Karaites persuaded many Jews to join them; especially those living in lands governed by Mohammedans. For years, the Karaites kept growing in numbers until it seemed as if they might win the majority of Jews to their side. At this time however, a young Egyptian Jew, learned in the Torah, Talmud, grammar, and Arabic was selected as Gaon of Sura and made the

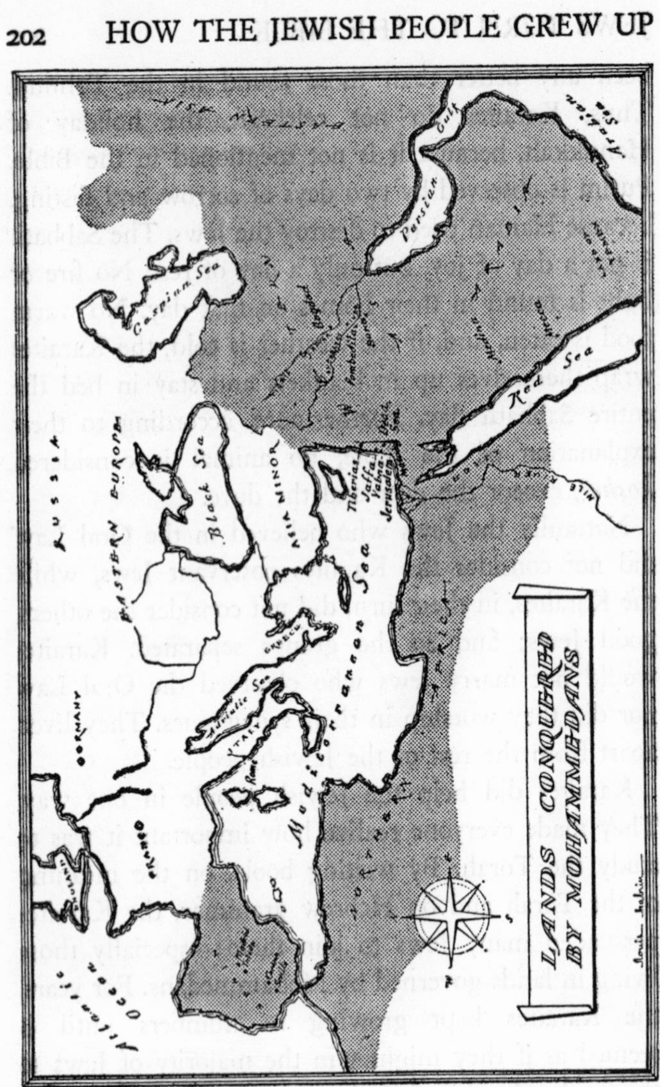
LANDS CONQUERED
BY MOHAMMEDANS
Caspian Sea
Black Sea
Red Sea
Persian Gulf
Mediterranean Sea
ASIA MINOR
EASTERN EUROPE
RUSSIA
GERMANY
FRANCE
ITALY
GREECE
Rome
Adriatic Sea
Atlantic Ocean
Tiberias
Jaffa
Jerusalem
Dead Sea
Pumbeditha
Mecca
Medina

people realize that though the Karaites were right in studying the Torah, they were wrong in dropping the study of the Oral Law. We shall learn about him in our next chapter.

Answer the questions to Topic IV.

ADDITIONAL READING

The Great March. The story of Samuel is dramatically retold in "As Faithful As That," on page 109–113.

Great Men In Israel. "In a Castle in Arabia," pages 49–54, repeats the story of Samuel.

SOMETHING TO THINK ABOUT

1. Were the Karaites right in their belief that only the Written Law was to be obeyed while the Oral Law as stated in the Talmud should be disregarded (dropped)? Why?
2. Did Anan ben David help or harm the Jewish people? Why?
3. Did the Jews help the Arabs as much as the Arabs helped them?

Why Were the Talmudical Colleges Closed?

AT PRESENT, Babylonia is only a name which we come upon in studying our history. Yet Babylonia was for a long, long time—for almost a thousand years —the very center of Jewish learning. Jews from Europe, Africa, or distant parts of Asia often came to Sura with questions about the meaning of Talmudical expressions or the proper observance of Jewish laws. What happened to the colleges and the scholars who crowded into them?

1. WHY DID THE COLLEGES LOSE THEIR IMPORTANCE?

From your last chapter, you will recall that many Jews became interested in the Bible and ceased to study the Talmud. Under the leadership of Anan ben David, they became Karaites and refused to obey the Oral Law entirely. Others continued to obey the Oral Law, but desired earnestly to study the Written Law. A third group of Jews became interested in the study of beautiful Arabic poetry, medicine, arithmetic, and other subjects which we now study in high schools and colleges.

None of these subjects were taught in the

Babylonian colleges. And so students left the Talmudical schools and found other places for pursuing the studies which interested them. The Geonim made no effort to bring back those who left. They refused to make any changes in the list of subjects to be taught; they did not try to show that the Karaites were wrong in disregarding the Oral Law; and they did nothing to win back those Jews who spent all their time on Arabic instead of Jewish learning.

Naturally the Colleges became less important to the Jewish people, and they did not support them as readily as before. The Geonim were then forced to send messengers to all parts of the world in order to collect money for the colleges.

Answer the Questions to Topic I of Chapter 19.

II. WHO WAS SAADIA?

Just about a thousand years ago, an Egyptian Jew, Saadia, was appointed Gaon of Sura. Everyone soon realized that the new Gaon was an extraordinary man. Before he was twenty-five, Saadia had already written many books. One was a Hebrew-Arabic dictionary, another was a book proving that the Karaites were mistaken, and a third settled an argument about the calendar between the leading Jews of Babylonia and Palestine. Before many more years had passed, Saadia had written a Hebrew grammar, and a translation of the Bible into Arabic which is still being used by the Yemenite Jews who speak only Arabic.

It was not the number of Saadia's books which

made him important, but their quality. His works showed that Saadia knew the Torah well, was a master of Arabic, and was thoroughly learned in the Talmud. His books were widely read and are still studied by Jewish scholars today. All who read the books wondered how one man could know so much. Even the Karaites were surprised to see how well Saadia knew the Torah and Hebrew grammar; and they had to admit, for the first time, that others besides Karaites knew the Torah.

Saadia was born in Egypt in 882, which is about 1050 years ago. Who taught him all he knew, no one can truly say. There were no great Jewish colleges in Egypt. In all likelihood, Saadia studied with private teachers, read all the good books in Hebrew, Arabic, and Aramaic that he could find, and thus learned a great deal about the Bible, Hebrew grammar, and the Talmud. From Arabic teachers, Saadia also learned what the wise men of the world thought about God and the universe, and how people should live in this world.

For some unknown reason, Saadia went to Palestine where he continued his studies. In the city of Tiberias, he found a number of scholars learned in the Bible and in Hebrew grammar. These men busied themselves in determining exactly how each word of the Bible should be written and pronounced. With their help, he perfected his knowledge of the Bible and Hebrew grammar. He then went on to Persia, where he studied, and, for a short time, taught, in the Pumbedita Talmudical College. He thus became a thorough master of the Talmud.

Answer the questions to Topic II.

III. HOW DID SAADIA HELP THE COLLEGE AT SURA?

But all his learning and wisdom would ordinarily not have been sufficient to raise him to the high office of Gaon. The Babylonian Jews were very proud of their Talmudical colleges. During the entire 700 years of the existence of Sura, since the days of the Amora Rab, no one but a Babylonian had ever stood at its head. What made it possible for an Egyptian Jew to become Gaon of a college where only Talmud was studied, and where only Babylonians taught? The truth is that the Resh Galuta was unable to find any other man. Many of the more learned men had died and no younger men had come to take their places. The last Gaon had been so poor that he had to work as a weaver by day in order to earn a living. This left him very little time for study. His knowledge was, therefore, little and his fame even less. During the time he served as Gaon of Sura, fewer students came to that college than had ever come before. No messengers came from distant lands to learn Jewish laws and customs. The college of Sura was no longer important or famous.

When this Gaon died, about 1000 years ago, there was no Babylonian Jew learned enough to become Gaon of Sura. The Resh Galuta feared that the college would have to close its doors. To save it, he invited

Saadia . . . devoted his time to writing.

Saadia, in spite of his Egyptian birth, to come to Sura and head the college. Saadia, who was then living in Palestine, felt greatly honored, and came at once.

With a man of Saadia's ability at the head of the college, students again began to come to Sura in great numbers. The subjects taught now were Bible and Hebrew grammar, in addition to Talmud. People came to study Talmud and Torah under the greatest Gaon that Sura had ever had. Jews from other lands again began coming to Sura with their questions and gifts, and thus helped support the college. For a time it seemed as though Babylonia might remain the center of Jewish life for many more years.

Answer the questions to Topic III.

IV. HOW WAS THE CENTER OF JEWISH LEARNING DESTROYED?

Then a quarrel broke out between the Resh Galuta and the Gaon of Sura. Thereupon, the Resh Galuta called together a large assembly in the synagogue of Sura, and announced that no one should visit Saadia or even talk with him. The Gaon was dismissed from Sura and was forced to live quietly in another city, Bagdad. Saadia, saddened by all that happened, devoted his time to writing.

His best book, *Beliefs and Opinions,* Saadia wrote in Bagdad at that time. In this important work, he pointed out that the Torah was a great book and deserved to be respected, even by people who had learned all the wisdom of the Arabs and who considered themselves wiser than the rest of the Jews. Yet Saadia did not agree with those who believed that it was wrong to study any other book than the Talmud or the Torah. He felt that people *ought to read* good books in addition to the Torah and Talmud. They could then more readily understand all that goes on in the world.

Seven years after his quarrel with the Resh Galuta, Saadia was recalled to Sura. However, he died only five years later. Saadia had been an exceptionally good scholar and a fine character. No one could be found to take his place as Gaon. As a result, the college was finally closed, a few years after his death.

With the closing of Sura, the center of Jewish life in Babylonia was broken up. No longer did the greatest scholars live there. No longer were the best colleges located in Babylonian cities. No longer did Jews living far away, come to Babylonia for guidance in their laws and customs or instruction in the meaning of difficult statements in the Talmud or Bible.

The break-up of the center of learning did not mean that all the Jews moved out of Babylonia. Many continued to live there, and some still do. For many years after the close of Sura, the college in Pumbedita continued to teach the Talmud. Fully a hundred years passed, before the doors of Pumbedita were finally closed. The Babylonian Jews did little to help Judaism after the death of Saadia. It was the European Jews, especially the Spanish, who took their place, and brought forth leaders worthy of our people. These new leaders and their manner of living are of interest to us, and we shall devote our attention to them. Our future lessons will concern themselves with the life of our people in the European lands.

Answer the questions to Topic IV.

ADDITIONAL READING

The Great March. The reason for the quarrel between Saadia and the Resh Galuta is told in the story, "Even Though I Lose," beginning on page 122.

Great Jews since Bible Times. "The Boy from Egypt," gives in brief the life story of Saadia. The story begins on page 41.

SOMETHING TO THINK ABOUT

1. What is meant by the expression: "The Center of Jewish Learning was broken up?"
2. Why was the Babylonian Center of Jewish Learning broken up?

How Did a Center for Judaism Arise in Western Europe?

Up to now, we have learned what happened to our people during the first three thousand years of their history. We think back over their hard life in the desert, their slavery in Egypt, their happiness and their achievements in Palestine. Lastly we recall how they developed the Talmud in Babylonia. During all those three thousand years, Europe was hardly known to the majority of the Jews. And yet, practically all of us now live in Europe or America with only a few hundred thousand in Palestine. The desert, Egypt, and Babylonia are only memories of days gone by! How did it happen that the center of Judaism was moved to Europe?

I. HOW DID THE JEWS LIVE IN EUROPE?

Small groups of our people came to Europe while our ancestors still lived in Palestine. When the Romans destroyed the Temple, over 1860 years ago, many more Jews fled from Palestine and came to Rome and other large European cities. Some of these men traveled for business reasons. When they found a good place in which to live, they settled there. Thus Jews came into the European lands now known as Italy, Spain, France, and Germany; a few reached England.

In Europe, some of our people became farmers, and a few turned soldiers; but the majority went into business.

Like their brethren in Palestine and Babylonia, the European Jews followed the Written and Oral Law as well as they could. The father generally taught his children how Jews should live and what laws they were to follow. Sometimes a teacher from Babylonia or Palestine helped to instruct the people. When no member in an entire congregation knew how to carry out a certain law, the group sent a messenger to the head of a Babylonian college, for information.

About 1200 years ago, the Christian ruler of Spain ordered the Jews living there to become Christians or leave the land. He threatened to make a slave of any Jew who remained. Some left Spain, a few became Christians; the majority pretended to accept Christianity, but remained secretly faithful to the Jewish religion. Fortunately, just at that time, the Mohammedans conquered Spain.

The new rulers treated the Jews well. They allowed them to live and work in peace and to follow out all the laws of their religion. Many more Jews then came to Spain from far-off Babylonia, Palestine, the countries of North Africa, and from other European lands. As the years went by the number of Jews in Spain kept increasing.

Since the Jews and Mohammedans were on friendly

terms, they learned many things from one another. Jews learned to speak, read, and write Arabic. In return, they taught the Arabs the contents of some of the finest Greek, Hebrew, and Latin books, by translating them into Arabic. The rulers of Spain, known as Caliphs, were well pleased with the work of the Jews and encouraged them to go on with their studies. The Jews also studied medicine, arithmetic, and astronomy (the science of the heavenly bodies). Again, as physicians, they used their knowledge to help Mohammedans as well as Jews; they healed the sick and added to the knowledge of both peoples.

Answer the questions to Topic I of Chapter 20.

II. WHAT MADE HASDAI FAMOUS?

About 1000 years ago, the Caliph of Spain appointed the Jew, Hasdai, as his personal doctor. He found him to be a good doctor and a very wise man. When the Caliph asked his advice on affairs of the government, Hasdai proved himself as good an advisor as he was a physician. The Caliph, therefore, discussed all his important problems with Hasdai. When ambassadors came from foreign lands, the Caliph invited his Jewish doctor to be present, and was pleased to see how quickly Hasdai put the ambassadors at their ease by speaking to them in a language which they understood. The Caliph then appointed Hasdai, his advisor, as well as his physician.

The Jews of Spain rejoiced to see one of their own people so highly honored by the Caliph. They were proud of him. Besides, they knew that they would not be made to suffer on account of their religion. They were right. Hasdai guarded the rights of the Jews in Spain and helped them build a new center for Judaism when the old one in Babylonia was broken up.

What did Hasdai actually do to help the Jewish people in Spain? In the first place, he helped make the small Talmudical college in the city of Cordova, famous. The Spanish scholars at that time knew so little of the Talmud, that when a difficult question arose concerning the meaning of a law, they were generally obliged to send a messenger to the Gaon of Sura or Pumbedita for the correct answer.

A fortunate incident helped Hasdai to make this college a fine one. According to a popular story, a Jewish slave was bought by the Jews of Cordova and set free. One day, he came to the Talmudical college and sat listening to the discussions. He heard a pupil ask the president of the college a question which the president was unable to answer. The redeemed slave asked for permission to speak. When it was granted, he answered the question to the satisfaction of all present. The president, in surprise, asked him who he was and where he had come from. The man replied that his name was Moses ben Hanokh and that he was a Babylonian Jew. He was, in fact, one of the rabbis who had been sent out by the colleges of Sura and Pumbedita to collect money for their support. When he was asked how he had happened to become

The redeemed slave asked for permission to speak.

a slave, Moses answered that the ship on which he had travelled had been captured by pirates, and all the passengers had been sold as slaves.

When the president of the college realized that Moses ben Hanokh was a learned Talmudical scholar from Babylonia, he resigned, and advised the people to elect ben Hanokh in his place. This was done, and Moses became the head of the college in Cordova. When Hasdai was told what a great scholar stood at the head of the college in Cordova, he gave a large sum of money to be used for purchasing more books, for supporting poor scholars, and for all the other expenses of the college. Copies of the Talmud were then brought to Spain from Babylonia, and the study of the Talmud was begun in earnest.

Answer the questions to Topic II.

III. HOW DID SPAIN BECOME THE CENTER OF JEWISH LEARNING?

Moses ben Hanokh himself did most of the teaching, which proved to be very successful. Like his Babylonian teachers, ben Hanokh would read a part of the Talmud and then explain it. After that he would permit all the students who did not fully understand his explanation, to ask questions. The questions were discussed by the students until each one felt that he knew the lesson perfectly. After some years of study, many students knew the Talmud well.

Some of these scholars returned to their home towns and themselves became teachers. Thus they spread the knowledge of the Talmudical laws (Halakhah) and stories (Aggada) among the Spanish Jews.

Jews living in all parts of Europe and North Africa soon heard of the excellent Talmudical college in Cordova and were greatly pleased. When they needed information on the Oral Law it was no longer necessary to go to Babylonia. The head of the college in Cordova could answer all their questions. Spain thus took the place of Babylonia, and Cordova became a center of Jewish learning, just as Sura had been in the days of the great Geonim.

Hasdai watched the Talmudical college grow, and felt pleased indeed. However, like the Gaon Saadia, he believed that learned people should read other good books besides the Torah and Talmud. But there were few other good books, at that time, which interested the Jews. Hasdai, therefore, chose a few men who were able to write good books and gave them enough money to live comfortably. Thus, he made it possible for them to spend their time in writing, instead of working in the field or in a store. These men prepared Hebrew grammars, books of poetry, and explanations of Jewish laws and customs. Thus, the knowledge of Judaism became widespread among the Jews in Spain.

Answer the questions to Topic III.

IV. WHAT INCREASED THE HAPPINESS OF THE SPANISH JEWS?

Because of his high position, Hasdai was able to help his people in another way. He protected them from danger of all kinds. Those unfriendly to the Jews dared not attack them, because they knew that Hasdai would have the Caliph punish them severely.

Hasdai protected the Jews living in other lands, also. He did this by asking the ambassadors who came to Spain from all over the world to be kind to his people. The ambassadors, eager to please Hasdai, urged the rulers of their countries to protect the Jews in case of danger.

One day, Hasdai found out from the ambassador of a far-off land, that a Jewish kingdom existed in Russia. He immediately sent a messenger to that Jewish king, with a letter written in Hebrew, asking about his kingdom. After some time, the reply finally reached Hasdai, and this is what it told him.

At about the same time that the Mohammedans had conquered Spain, the king of a people, called Khazars, had become dissatisfied with worshipping idols, and had become a Jew. A great many of his lords, generals, and soldiers had done likewise. Rabbis were then invited to come and teach Jewish laws and customs to the Jewish Khazars. During the two hundred years of the existence of this Jewish kingdom, most of the Khazars had learned the Jewish religion and were living in accordance with its laws.

Hasdai rejoiced greatly to learn of the kingdom of the Khazars. Unfortunately, the Russians destroyed it a few years later. You are probably wondering: "What happened to the Jewish Khazars?" Some of them mingled with the other Jews of Russia, and the others

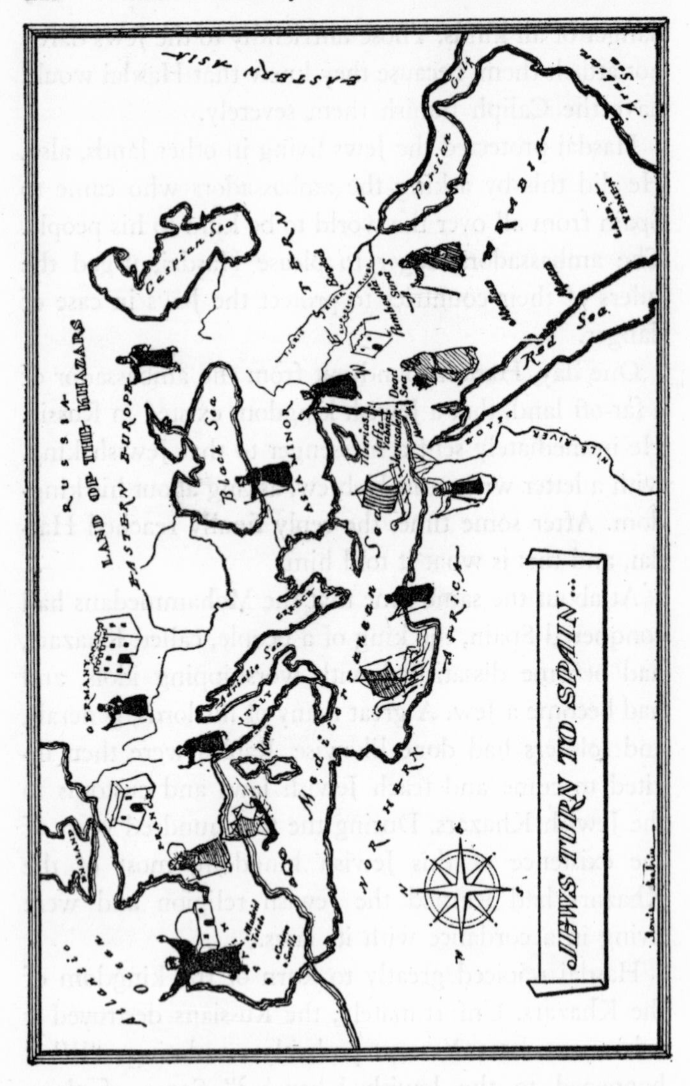
JEWS TURN TO SPAIN...
EASTERN ASIA
Persian Gulf
ARABIA
LAND OF YEMEN
Caspian Sea
RUSSIA
LAND OF THE KHAZARS
EASTERN EUROPE
Black Sea
ASIA MINOR
Baghdad
Pumbeditha
Sura
Medina
Mecca
Red Sea
Dead Sea
Tiberias
Jaffa
Jerusalem
EGYPT
NILE RIVER
GREECE
Adriatic Sea
ITALY
Rome
GERMANY
FRANCE
ENGLAND
Mediterranean Sea
NORTHERN AFRICA
Madrid
Toledo
Cordova
Seville
Atlantic Ocean

gradually forgot their Judaism and became Christians.

Hasdai was grieved to learn that the Jewish kingdom of the Khazars, like that of the Yemenites, had been destroyed. However, he could not restore it. And so he once more turned his attention to the Jewish center in Spain.

By this time there were many great poets, scholars, and travellers among the Spanish Jews. When Hasdai died, Spain was the land in which the most learned Jews were to be found. Those, elsewhere, who wanted to know about their religious and their holy books, now turned to Spain for information, just as they had once turned to Babylonia. Spain had become the new center of Judaism. For five hundred years, the Jewish center in Spain continued to develop and to grow more famous. Scholars, poets, and thinkers appeared at that time who were greater than many of the men whom we have discussed. In the coming chapters we shall study about some of them.

Answer the questions to Topic IV.

ADDITIONAL READING

The Great March. "A Gift to the Caliph" tells of Hasdai and his skill in languages. The story is worth reading. It is found on pages 126–130. "The Choice," on pages 131–136 tells an interesting legend explaining how the Khazars became Jews. "The Slave Rabbi," tells about . . . well, you ought to know! Read the story! It begins on page 137.

Great Men in Israel. "The Prince of Cordova," repeats the story of Hasdai's life. Read it if you have time. It begins on page 55.

Great Jews since Bible Times. "Four Rabbis Who Went to Spain," tells the legend of ben Hanokh. It begins on page 45. "The Far Away Kingdom," on pages 50–52, tells about the Khazars.

SOMETHING TO THINK ABOUT

1. Give your reasons why Jews should have been able to translate books from one language to another more easily than their learned Arabic neighbors.
2. What did Hasdai do to help develop Spain as a center of Jewish learning?

How Did Jews Live under the Rule of Christians?

N Spain, the Jews lived happily under the rule of the Mohammedan Caliphs. But in the rest of Europe, especially in France, Germany, and England, where Christian kings, princes, and high officers were in control, our people were not happy.

1. HOW DID THE JEWS LIVE UNDER CHRISTIAN RULERS?

The Christians, in their desire to make all people believe in Jesus, made life unbearable for those who did not so believe. For this reason, Jews were forbidden to have Christian slaves or even servants. They were not allowed to serve as officers of the kings and princes. They even had difficulty in getting land on which they could earn a living by farming.

The Jews could do nothing to change these unfair laws. And, besides, as most of them were engaged in business, they were able to earn a comfortable living. Of course, they gave their children as good an education as possible. They taught them Torah and Talmud, but very few other subjects.

Educating children was much more difficult then, than it is today. The majority of the people did not realize that education was necessary. Even kings and princes could barely sign their names. Ordinary folks could not read or write a word. And yet, a French Jew who lived at that time, became one of the greatest Talmudical scholars in the world. The explanations he wrote about 850 years ago, are still used today by all who study the Talmud.

That scholar was *Ra*bbi *Sh*elomoh ben *I*saac, generally known by his initials as *Rashi*. He was born in the year 1040 which is almost 900 years ago. Legends grew up about Rashi, as they always do about famous people. One story tells that Rashi's father, a dealer in precious stones, possessed a very large and beautiful diamond. Some Christians wanted to buy it from him, and were willing to pay a high price for it. But when he found out that they wanted to use it for a statue in their church, he refused to sell it. Then one day as he was walking along the banks of the river, he was asked to step into a boat for a ride, and accepted the invitation. But when he sat down, he noticed that the people who had wanted to buy his stone were there. He immediately turned to get off the boat, but saw that he was already too far from shore. As he expected, the Christians again offered to buy the diamond, and threatened to throw him into the river, if he refused to sell. To save himself, he threw the jewel into the water. Though the men were deeply disappointed, they did the merchant no harm. When he returned home, sick at heart over his loss, the good Jew heard a voice which said: "A son will be born to you who will be more brilliant than the diamond which you have just lost." Shelomoh was born a year later.

Answer the questions to Topic I of Chapter 21.

II. HOW WAS RASHI EDUCATED?

Shelomoh ben Isaac (*Rashi*) began to study the Torah when he was barely six. His own father was his first teacher. Under his direction, the little fellow was kept busy at his studies from morning until evening. In a few years he had learned the Hebrew language, as well as the contents of the Bible. He then began to study Talmud. At first, this subject seemed very difficult. Young Shelomoh had to learn a new language, Aramaic, in addition to Hebrew; there were no punctuation marks to help him; at times the words did not seem to make sense and at other times there did not seem to be any connection between one sentence and another. His father, however, was a patient teacher, and the child was a very bright and willing pupil. In addition, Talmud was practically the only subject of study besides the Torah. And so the boy soon found the work easier and more interesting. After a number of years, the study of the Talmud proved so interesting that the lad decided to devote his whole life to it.

When he was eighteen years old, Shelomoh ben Isaac left his home town and went to other cities in France and Germany, where he studied under the greatest Talmudists of his time. Since he had no regular way of making a living, Shelomoh often suffered from hunger, thirst, and cold, and depended largely on the help of kind people. Nevertheless, he continued his studies.

To make sure that he would remember what he learned, the young student kept notes on loose pieces of paper and in notebooks. In order to write quickly, he invented a simple way of making the letters of the alphabet. He made them very small and shaped them a little differently from the letters of the regular Hebrew alphabet. As a result, Rashi's notes look so different from ordinary printed Hebrew that people who desire to read them must spend some time in becoming familiar with the new alphabet.

Answer the questions to Topic II.

WHAT MADE RASHI GREAT?

After years of study and suffering, Rabbi Shelomoh ben Isaac finally returned to his home town. There he was honored with the title of "rabbi and teacher" and became known as *Rashi.* His knowledge of the Talmud was so complete, that he soon became more famous than any of the Talmudical scholars of Spain or Babylonia had ever been. Young men came to study under his guidance and people turned to him with questions concerning Jewish customs and laws, instead of going to Babylonia or Spain.

Rashi's fame, however, is not due to his excellence as a teacher but to his written explanations of the Talmud and Torah. He began this work when he was still a young man, and continued it to the very end of

The little fellow was kept busy at his studies from morning until evening.

his life. Rashi's explanations are simple and clear. Sometimes he makes a very difficult sentence easy to understand by merely proving that the scribe had not copied it correctly. At other times, he translates a word into French. Then again, Rashi often simplifies a Talmudical discussion by explaining what the Tannaim and the Amoraim meant.

These explanations, Rashi was constantly able to improve by trying them on his pupils. Those which did not help the students were changed for better ones. To make the study of Talmud and Torah more interesting, he often introduced a beautiful little story. As a result, Rashi's notes on the Talmud became well-known and widely used even in his own lifetime. Nowadays, no one studies the Talmud without reading Rashi's writings. Every copy of the Talmud now contains his famous explanations printed in the alphabet which he himself had made up.

Rashi's notes on the Torah are even more widely known than those on the Talmud. However, this is not because they are better, but rather because the Torah is read and studied much more than the Talmud.

In spite of his fame as a scholar, and his honored position as a rabbi and teacher, Rashi had to earn a living by growing grapes and working on a farm. He earned very little—just enough for his food, his clothes, and a home. But he was content, because he was able to study, to teach, and to write. However, the last ten years of Rashi's life were saddened by a series of dreadful attacks on the Jews of France, Germany, and England. Here is what happened.

Answer the questions to Topic III.

IV. WHAT BROUGHT SUFFERING ON THE JEWS?

The chief of the priests, called the "pope," asked all the Christians to arm themselves, march to Palestine, and take the holy land away from the Mohammedans. A large number of soldiers assembled in France and Germany to prepare for war (generally known as a Crusade) against the Mohammedans. A wicked man then told the warriors (called Crusaders), that the Jews had killed Jesus and should be made to suffer for it. The Crusaders attacked the Jews of Germany and France, killed thousands of them, destroyed their homes and property, made beggars of those who escaped with their lives, and forced hundreds of them to become Christians.

Rashi himself was not harmed, but his heart was filled with pain when he saw how cruelly his fellow Jews were being treated. He died soon after.

After Rashi's death, Jewish life in European countries outside of Spain, became even harder to bear. The first war with the Mohammedans was not entirely successful. So the pope called for a second Crusade, and then a third, a fourth, and a fifth Crusade. Each time a new war was started against the Mohammedans in Palestine, the Christian soldiers, on their march to the holy land, attacked the European Jews, killing, robbing, burning, and destroying.

But this was not all. Time and again, the kings declared that Christians who owed money to Jews did not have to pay it back. At the same time, they commanded the Jews to pay them large sums of money in taxes. Naturally the Jews became poor. When the kings found that they were unable to squeeze any more money out of the Jews, they drove them out altogether. They had to leave England in 1290 (about 650 years ago), and they were driven from France a hundred years later, in 1394.

Yet more suffering was to come to the Jews of Europe. In Germany and Italy, where Jews were still permitted to live, they could dwell only in special districts of certain cities. Each Jew had to wear a yellow badge, so that everybody might know he was a Jew. Christians meeting Jews often struck them with sticks or stones, without fear of punishment. Some times they attacked whole communities of Jews.

All sorts of excuses were given for the attacks. The one used most often was that Jews had killed a Christian lad before Passover and put his blood into the mazzot! Can you imagine anything so stupid? And yet some people believed it. Without stopping to find out whether the story was true, large crowds of ruffians attacked the Jews, robbed them, destroyed their homes, and burned many of them alive. This did not happen just once, but many times, and rarely did the police protect the Jews. They usually joined the crowds who attacked the Jews! So persistently did the Christians believe this terrible lie, that, barely twenty years ago, a Russian Jew, named Mendel Beilis, was accused of murdering a Christian child and using his blood for baking mazzot! The poor man suffered many years of imprisonment before he was freed of this ridiculous charge. He came to America, where he soon died because his health had been ruined.

A great plague, called the Black Plague, which broke out about 600 years ago and brought death to millions of people in Europe, served as another excuse for attacking the Jews. The Jews were accused of causing this terrible disease by poisoning the wells. Christians all over Europe attacked the helpless and defenseless Jews and murdered them by the hundreds.

Despite this harsh treatment, Jews continued to live in Germany and Italy. They had to earn a living either by buying and selling second-hand goods or by lending money at interest. Neither method made it possible for them to earn enough with which to live comfortably. But they struggled on, hoping that some day God would put an end to their troubles.

They had one comfort—the study of the Torah and the Talmud. But even in this, the Jews were disturbed. The king of France once had all the copies of the Talmud collected and burnt, leaving the poor Jews without even their Talmud. But after a time, other copies were procured and learning went on. When they lost themselves in their books, the people were able to forget their many troubles and dream of a time when they would all be happy again.

Answer the questions to Topic IV.

ADDITIONAL READING

The Great March. "Not for His Crown," tells a story about a jewel, but it is not the same as you read in your lesson. Read this one. It begins on page 191.

"How Rashi Was Saved," is an interesting legend about the great scholar. Read it for yourself and see. It begins on page 196.

"The Fourth Horse," is a curious story dealing with the Crusades. It begins on page 201.

Great Men in Israel. "In the Name of God," tells how Crusaders dealt with Jews. The story begins on page 77.

"Why a Rich Man Went Hungry," repeats the legend of the "lost jewel." The story begins on page 84.

"The Rabbi and the Bishop," tells how by a deed of kindness, the rabbi saved himself from trouble. The story begins on page 87.

Great Jews since Bible Times. Read "How Rashi Saved His People"—pages 54–58, and "Pilgrims to Palestine," on pages 59–63.

SOMETHING TO THINK ABOUT

1. Why did Christians want the Jews to live in special districts? Did Jews like it? Why?
2. Why is Rashi better known among Jews than the Gaon Saadia or the advisor to the Caliph, Hasdai?
3. Why was it harder to become learned in France than in Spain?

How Did They Live in Spain?

THE Jews living in the western and central parts of Europe were murderously attacked, driven out of their homes, forced into ghettoes, made to wear yellow badges, prevented from earning a living in an honorable way, and disturbed even in their study of the holy books. But in Spain they were treated well and fairly.

I. WHAT IS MEANT BY "THE GOLDEN AGE"?

So great a difference existed between the life of the Jews in Spain and that of those in the rest of Europe, that the suffering ones could not believe the reports from Spain. When a German Jewish community heard that, in Spain, a Jew served as the Caliph's highest officer, the people thought it was just the invention of some poor fellow whose troubles had driven him mad. But it was no fairy tale. Hasdai did hold that office, and other Jews also reached that high position. In addition, many Jews were officers of the government, possessed much wealth and learning, practiced medicine, wrote books, and composed poetry.

From time to time, wars broke out in Spain. Mo-

A Jew served as the Caliph's highest officer, . . .

hammedan princes fought with each other and divided the country into a great many little states. The Christians took advantage of the quarrels among the Mohammedans and slowly but steadily reconquered large parts of the land. Naturally, everybody suffered from these wars. But the Jews suffered no more than the others, and when peace was restored, they quickly regained what they had lost in the wars.

In a way, the constant fighting between Christians and Mohammedans helped the Jews. Because each side wanted their friendship, both treated them well and fairly. And so it happened that Christian rulers in Spain protected the Jews, while those in other lands treated them very harshly.

Thanks to the kind treatment of the Spanish rulers, Jews were able to live happily. They worshipped God in beautiful synagogues and studied the Torah and the Talmud in their schools and colleges. In addition, many Jews attended the Spanish universities, where they studied Spanish, Arabic, poetry, the wise sayings of all great and learned men, medicine, and many other subjects which you, too, may learn when you get to college.

Jewish scholars in Spain thus knew, not only Talmud and Torah, but also how to write poetry and how to heal the sick. In southern Spain, the Jewish advisor of the Mohammedan ruler was also a teacher in the Talmudical college, and a poet. He even wrote some of his letters in poetry.

Because the Spanish Jews at that time were so happy,

so well educated, and wrote so many excellent books, we still call those days "The Golden Age."

Answer the questions to Topic I of Chapter 22.

II. WHO WAS THE FINEST POET OF THE GOLDEN AGE?

The greatest and most interesting Jewish poet who lived during the Golden Age was Judah Halevi. He was born about 850 years ago in the city of Toledo, located in the middle of Spain. When he was young, he studied Torah and Talmud with his father. In addition, young Judah also studied the Hebrew language and its grammar. This language he learned so well that he used it in writing his poems, though the languages he spoke were Arabic and Spanish.

At the age of thirteen, Judah began to study medicine, in the practice of which he later earned his living. At the same time he studied the methods and rules of writing poetry. He also learned about the stars, and studied arithmetic and other subjects now taught in our high schools and colleges. In addition, Judah continued his study of the Torah, the Talmud, and the Hebrew language.

Judah did not take up these subjects in his home town. Instead, he went to Cordova. There he studied in the great Talmudical college made famous by Moses ben Hanokh. But Judah was not as much interested in Talmud as in poetry, and often spent his time writing poetry or riddles instead of studying Talmud. One of his riddles is the following:

"What is it that is blind, with an eye in its head,

and the rest of mankind its use cannot spare; spends all its life in clothing the dead and always itself is naked and bare?" Can you guess what it is? Think hard. It is . . . a needle!

After many years of study, spent far away from his home, Judah Halevi returned to Toledo. Though he earned his living by practicing medicine, this did not absorb all his attention. What interested him most was his poetry. Judah was a person who felt things deeply and expressed his feelings in poetry. Some of the best known poets of his time praised his work and encouraged him to continue writing. Judah also wrote a famous book on Judaism, called the "Kusari."

One of his friends, knowing how well Judah wrote, asked him to write a poem in honor of his wedding. Judah did as his friend asked. The poem pleased every one so well that many people came to Judah for poems celebrating special events, such as engagements or weddings. They also asked him to write poems in honor of beloved people who died.

Judah wrote such poems by the hundreds and he soon became famous throughout Spain. Today, however, we remember him because he wrote many beautiful songs about Palestine. We remember him because he was "The Sweet Singer of Zion."

Answer the questions to Topic II.

III. WHAT ARE SOME OF JUDAH HALEVI'S POEMS?

Judah's poetry showed a deep love for God, his people, and their ancient homeland. Many of his poems were even included in the prayerbook and are still recited in our services.

Here is a poem written by Judah Halevi, showing his love for God. The hard words are explained directly below.

THE PRIDE OF A JEW

With all my heart, in truth, and passion[1] strong,
I love Thee; both in solitude[2] and throng[3]
Thy name's with me, alone I shall not bide![4]
My friend art Thou, though others from me glide.[5]
My lamp art Thou; my light shall never fade,[6]
Nor shall my foot e'er slip, by Thee upstayed.[7]
They little knew who have despised[8] me so,
That shaming me doth cause my pride to glow.
O Fountain[9] of my life, I'll bless Thee aye,[10]
And sing Thy praises, O my song, alway!

—*Translated by* ISRAEL COHEN

Meaning of Difficult Words

1 Feeling.
2 When I am all alone.
3 When I am in the midst of a crowd.
4 Stay.
5 Go away.
6 Go out.
7 Helped; supported.
8 Looked down upon.
9 God.
10 Forever.

Here is an example of a poem which Judah wrote, showing his love for his people, and expressing his belief that they will live forever, in spite of all their troubles.

THE IMMORTALITY[1] OF ISRAEL

The sun and moon unchanging[2] do obey
The laws that never cease[3] or night or day.
Appointed[4] signs are they to Jacob's seed
That life eternal[5] hath been them decreed.[6]
And, though, O Lord, Thy left hand dealeth[7] pain,
Thy right shall lead them back to joy again.
Let not despair oppress[8] their quailing[9] heart.
Though radiant[10] fortune from their midst depart.
But let this constant faith their souls uphold.
That in the Book of Life their name's enrolled
For all eternity:[11] nor shall they cease
While night and day do alternate in peace.

—*Translated by* ISRAEL COHEN.

Meaning of Difficult Words

[1] Everlasting life.
[2] Always.
[3] Stop.
[4] Definite, sure.
[5] Everlasting.
[6] Given.
[7] Gives.
[8] Trouble.
[9] Filled with fear.
[10] Bright and good.
[11] Forever.

These are beautiful poems and now read the following two poems, showing his love for Zion. Think of it! Judah was living very comfortably in beautiful sunny Spain far to the west of Palestine. Yet he wanted to go to Palestine, which was then almost deserted.

OH! CITY OF THE WORLD

Oh! City of the world, most chastely[1] fair;
In the far west, behold I sigh[2] for thee.
And in my yearning[3] love I do bethink me

Of bygone ages; of thy ruined fane,[4]
The vanished[5] splendor of a vanished day.
Oh! Had I eagles' wings I'd fly to thee
And with my falling tears make moist thine
earth.
I long for thee; what though indeed thy kings
Have passed forever; though where once uprose
Sweet balsam trees, the serpent makes his nest.[6]
Oh! that I might embrace thy dust, the sod[7]
Were sweet as honey to my fond desire.

—*Translated by* KATE MAGNUS.

Meaning of Difficult Words

[1] Pure and beautiful.
[2] Long.
[3] Longing.
[4] Temple.
[5] Departed.
[6] The serpent makes his nest in a place where there are no people.
[7] Earth.

MY HEART IS IN THE EAST[1]

My heart is in the East, tho' in the West I live,
The sweet[2] of human life no happiness can give,
Religion's duties fail to lift my soul on high;
'Neath Edom[3] Zion writhes,[4] in Arab chains I lie!
No joy in sunny Spain mine eyes can ever see
For Zion, desolate,[5] alone hath charms for me!

—*Translated by* H. PEREIRA MENDES.

[1] Palestine is far east of Spain.
[2] Good things.
[3] Rome.
[4] Struggles.
[5] Deserted.

Answer the questions to Topic III.

IV. JUDAH VISITS PALESTINE

So strong and so real was Judah's love for the ancient homeland of our people that he finally decided to leave Spain and go to Palestine. It meant giving up a beautiful and comfortable home; it meant leaving his friends, his relatives, and his only daughter; it meant risking his life! Yet he went.

Judah boarded a ship which took him across the Mediterranean Sea to Egypt. There he found fellow-Jews living peacefully under a kindly Mohammedan ruler. When they found out who their guest was, they begged him to remain with them instead of going on to Palestine. The Jews pointed out that Jerusalem had been captured by Christians who did not permit any Jews to enter the city. Judah, however, refused to listen to them. He did not change his mind even when he learned that the Christians had burnt alive every Jew in Jerusalem and had forbidden the Jews to enter the city. And so, after a short stay in Egypt, he journeyed on to Palestine. He visited a few cities on the way to Jerusalem. But Judah never entered the city which he loved so much. He died without actually seeing Zion.

No one really knows how he died. One story tells that he reached the city of Jerusalem. In great joy, he threw himself on the ground and kissed the dust of the Holy Land. A soldier rode by at that moment and trampled the Sweet Singer of Zion to death.

Judah Halevi's death was mourned wherever Jews

Judah boarded a ship which took him across the Mediterranean Sea to Egypt.

lived, and his poems have never lost their charm. Many other poets, doctors, and scholars appeared who brought glory and greatness to the Jews and Spaniards alike, but the brilliance and the fame of the Sweet Singer of Zion never were surpassed.

Answer the questions to Topic IV.

ADDITIONAL READING

The Great March. During the "Golden Age" in Spain there were many poets and writers who lived about the same time as Judah. One very famous poet was Ibn Gabirol. A very interesting legend is told of him in "The Wondrous Tree," beginning on page 144. About Judah himself, you can read on pages 153–159. About Ibn Ezra read the story "An Angel Did It," beginning on page 160.

Great Men in Israel. The same three stories told in *The Great March* may be found in this book. About Ibn Gabirol read the story "The Jews and Their Arabian Neighbors," on pages 66–69. "A Lover of Zion," pages 70–73 tells about Judah, and the "Globe-Trotter," on pages 74–76 describes Ibn Ezra.

Great Jews since Bible Times. "At the Gates of Jerusalem," pages 64–68 is the story of Judah Halevi, while "The Happy Traveler," pages 69–72 tells about Ibn Ezra.

SOMETHING TO THINK ABOUT

1. Why did we speak of the time when poets like Judah Halevi lived in Spain, as "The Golden Age"?

2. Think of what you learned in the lesson before and try to answer these questions:
   (a) How old was Rashi when Judah Halevi was born?
   (b) What dreadful events took place in countries ruled by Christians a few years later? Now can you think of another reason why people spoke of that period in Spain as "The Golden Age"?
3. Do you think Halevi earned the title "Sweet Singer of Zion"? How did he earn it?

Who Was the Greatest Scholar of the "Golden Age"?

IN THE year 1135, almost exactly 800 years ago, a son was born to the rich and learned Maimon, leader of the Jewish community of Cordova. The boy, named Moses ben Maimon, generally known as Maimonides, grew to be the greatest Jewish scholar of the "Golden Age" in Spain. People still say in speaking of him: "From Moses to Moses, there was none like unto Moses." By this expression, they mean that Moses Maimonides was not only the greatest Jew of his time, but that he was also greater and more worthy of respect than any Jew that had ever lived, except the first Moses himself.

In 1935, people all over the world celebrated his 800th birthday. They held meetings, wrote books, and discussed his life and work.

I. WHEN MOSES WAS YOUNG

Let us see how the "Second Moses" became so great a scholar and what he did with his extraordinary knowledge and wisdom.

Moses was born at a time when it was easy to acquire a good education. There were many elementary schools to which Jewish boys might go; and there were private teachers for those who could afford to pay for them. There was a Talmudical College in Cordova, and Arab universities were to be found throughout the land. Moreover, people at that time realized the value of educating their children. They taught them not only Torah, Talmud, and Hebrew grammar, but also the subjects that you study in public schools. It was the "Golden Age" when Judah Halevi still lived.

Moses' first teacher was his father, Maimon. When he was still very young, Moses began to study the Talmud. He was so fine a student that nothing was too hard for him. He made such rapid progress that his father quickly realized that this son was to become a great scholar. He engaged other men to teach his son medicine, mathematics, astronomy, and other important subjects studied by learned men in Spain during the Golden Age. There was just one subject in which Moses Maimonides took no interest—poetry. Unlike Judah Halevi and other famous men of that time, Moses made no effort to write poetry.

Answer the questions to Topic I of Chapter 23.

II. MAIMONIDES WANDERS TO NORTH AFRICA

When Moses was only 13 years old, the Mohammedan ruler of Southern Spain was defeated by the Mohammedan king of North Africa. The new ruler disliked Jews as well as Christians and ordered them all to become Mohammedans. Many synagogues which had stood in Spain for hundreds of years were destroyed, and large numbers of Jews were forced to leave the country.

But where could the Jews go at that time? Europe was in the hands of Christians who hated the Jews. North Africa was in the hands of the same Mohammedan ruler who had conquered Spain. Even Palestine was closed to the Jews because it was being ruled by a Christian.

Many Jews pretended to be Mohammedans, though they practised their religion at home, where nobody could see them. Others went to Northern Spain which was in the hands of the Christian kings who treated Jews fairly. The rest became wanderers, who went about from place to place seeking a new home.

The family of Maimonides refused to make believe that they were Mohammedans or Christians. They, therefore, left their native city, and went to other places where they were, for a while, unknown. As soon as they became known, they left again and went elsewhere. Finally, Maimonides and his family left Spain altogether and went to one of the countries in Northern Africa.

During all his wanderings, Maimonides continued his studies. Since he could not easily get books, he had to rely on his good memory. But so wonderfully well did he remember what he had learned, that he even succeeded in writing some books during his travels, though he was then less than twenty years old.

In his new home in North Africa, Maimonides

He made his way to a ship and fled to Palestine.

found a great many Jews pretending to be Mohammedans. He knew why they did so, and did not ask them to live openly as Jews. Instead, he advised them to follow secretly as many of the Jewish laws as they could. Those Jews who had already forgotten Hebrew were told to pray in Arabic rather than not at all. So great was his reputation even at this early age, that the North African Jews followed his advice without question.

A certain rabbi, however, disagreed with young Maimonides. He announced that Jews who made believe they were Mohammedans by reciting the Mohammedan prayer "God is one and Mohammed is his prophet," should no longer be considered Jews. A number of Jews then gave up their religion altogether and became Mohammedans.

Maimonides knew that the Jews recited the Mohammedan prayer only to save their lives. He, therefore, wrote a letter to the leaders of those Jews who were pretending to have adopted Mohammedanism, and told them not to give up their Judaism, even if they could not obey *all* the Jewish laws. He assured them that it was better to break a few laws than suffer death or give up Judaism completely. The letter comforted the "Jewish Mohammedans" and led some of them to announce that they were really Jews. When the Mohammedan officers found out about the letter, they wanted to arrest Maimonides. However, he made his way to a ship and fled to Palestine.

Answer the questions to Topic II.

III. MAIMONIDES SETTLES IN EGYPT

It took Maimonides a whole month to cross the Mediterranean Sea. But after he arrived in Palestine, he did not stay there long. Life in Palestine was very hard because the Christians did not want Jews there, and only a few were able to escape the watchful eyes of the Christian officials and soldiers. Before leaving Palestine, however, Maimonides and his family visited the "Wailing Wall" which is part of one of the walls which once surrounded the Temple, and offered a prayer to God. Jews have been doing this since the Temple was destroyed. Only a few years ago, however, there was serious trouble in Palestine because Arabs did not let Jews pray at the "Wailing Wall," even though they had been doing so ever since the Temple was destroyed. The matter was finally settled by a special committee of important men who declared that the Wall belonged to the Arabs, but that the Jews had the right to worship there.

When Moses Maimonides left Palestine, he went to Egypt. There he found the Jews living happily under the rule of a Mohammedan Caliph, who was very friendly to them. The Jews were permitted to rule themselves. At their head was the "Nagid" (prince). Like the Babylonian Resh Galuta, the Egyptian Nagid was responsible for collecting the taxes which the Jews owed to the Caliph. The Nagid was also expected to make sure that there was peace among the Jews.

Although there was a large group of Jews living in Egypt at that time, they were not nearly as well educated as their Spanish brethren. There were no learned Talmudists among them, nor were there any gifted Jewish poets in their midst. Therefore, when the learned Moses Maimonides came to Egypt, he appeared as great in the eyes of the Egyptian Jews as Moses of old.

Answer the questions to Topic III.

IV. HOW MAIMONIDES BECAME "THE SECOND MOSES"

Maimonides did a great deal to earn the title of "The Second Moses." In the first place, he helped to spread the knowledge of the Jewish laws not only among the Egyptian Jews, but also among those living in all other parts of the world. People came to him with questions as they had once come to the Geonim in Babylonia, to ben Hanokh in Spain, and to Rashi in France. Maimonides himself wrote the answers to the questions and sent them to those who had asked for the information.

Answering questions was, however, only one way of teaching his people. Maimonides wrote three famous books which have, since then, been translated into many languages.

His first book, called *The Light,* is an explanation of the Mishnah. Maimonides found that most of the Jews living in lands ruled by Mohammedans knew only Arabic, and found Judah's Mishnah hard to understand. He therefore explained it in Arabic and incidentally added a very important chapter, telling what all loyal Jews were expected to believe. These "beliefs" are still printed in many of the Siddurim (prayerbooks).

The second book, *Mishneh Torah,* contains the entire Oral Law and is arranged in a manner which makes it easy for people to find a particular law in which they are interested.

The third book, Maimonides wrote only for scholars. He found many learned men who did not believe some important parts of the Torah. Some of these people seemed ready to give up their Judaism because certain parts of the Bible were not reasonable in their eyes.

Maimonides was not shocked by these people. He remembered that the Gaon Saadia had also found many Jews who did not believe certain parts of the Torah. He, therefore, wrote a book which he named, *Guide for the Perplexed* (people who are in doubt). In his *Guide* Maimonides tried to prove that everything in the Bible is reasonable if one only thinks hard and tries his best to find the real meaning of the words of the Bible.

These three books became known very quickly and were read by hundreds of people. Many rabbis felt that, in his books, Maimonides was too careful not to hurt the feelings of people who did not believe in the Torah. A few even accused Maimonides himself of not believing everything written in the Bible. They, therefore, felt that his books did more harm than good, and said that his *Guide* led people to disbelieve rather than believe in the Torah.

When one of his pupils told Maimonides what some of his enemies had said, Maimonides simply answered,

"I am too busy to spend my time teaching fools. Such people are not worthy of receiving an answer."

This was quite true, of course, and his refusal to argue with those who disagreed with him, made Maimonides even greater in the eyes of most of the Jews. When some of his enemies wrote books to show why the works of Maimonides should not be read, his friends wrote replies. Thus many new books appeared. Some praised Maimonides, while others spoke ill of him. People continued writing about him long after his death.

Most people, however, felt and still feel that Maimonides was one of the greatest Jewish scholars that ever lived. They felt that his explanations of the laws made it possible for them to observe the laws and customs more correctly and with a clearer understanding of their meaning. For that reason, they felt that he deserved to be called "The Second Moses."

There was another reason why they called Maimonides "The Second Moses." After staying in Egypt for some time, Maimonides became the recognized leader of all Jews, the world over. Furthermore, Maimonides taught Torah not only by answering questions and writing books, but also by preaching in the synagogue. Maimonides, you see, was also a rabbi.

Answer the questions to Topic IV.

V. MAIMONIDES AS DOCTOR

Since Maimonides was so busy writing books, answering questions, preaching, and leading his community, you may wonder how he earned a living. This he did, by practising medicine.

Moses Maimonides was no ordinary doctor. He knew how to cure people as well as to teach the observance of the laws of Judaism. He wrote books on medicine which were used long after his death. Famous doctors came to him for medical advice from far and near. The ruler of Egypt thought so well of Maimonides as a physician, that he employed him as his personal doctor.

Moses Maimonides was an unusually busy man. He spent his whole morning in the palace. In the afternoon Maimonides treated patients in his home. You will wonder how he found time for so much work! The answer is very simple. He ate only one meal a day, and went to bed only when he was too tired to do any more work.

The Sabbath was his only time for rest. But even then, Maimonides preached in the synagogue, consulted with the leaders of the Jewish community, and studied the Torah. He was a hard worker, in addition to being a brilliant man.

Did Maimonides deserve to be called the "Second Moses"?

What do *you* think?

Answer the questions to Topic V.

He earned a living by practicing medicine.

ADDITIONAL READING

Prayerbook. In the *Union Prayerbook* (for the High Holy Days) there are two selections from the writings of Maimonides. The first begins on page 297; the second, on page 299. The last is especially interesting in these hard times and is not difficult to understand. Read it.

The famous "Thirteen Principles of Faith" prepared by Maimonides are found in the *Authorized Daily Prayer Book* on pages 89–90.

The Great March. "The Doctor Arrives," on pages 169–174, and "Tables Turned," on pages 175–183 will make interesting reading.

Great Men in Israel. Read: "A Physician and His Pen of Truth," on pages 91–99.

Great Jews since Bible Times. Read "Moses Maimonides, the Good Doctor," on pages 74–78.

SOMETHING TO THINK ABOUT

1. Why did Maimonides settle in Egypt rather than in Palestine, Spain, France, or Germany?
2. Do you think Maimonides deserved to be called "The Second Moses"? Why?

What Was the First Sign of Trouble?

WHILE the Jews of southern Spain were, like Maimonides, forced to leave the country, those in northern Spain continued to live peacefully under their Christian rulers. At that time, 700 years ago, it was the only country in Europe where Jews were given fair treatment.

I. HOW JEWS LIVED IN SPAIN AND OUTSIDE OF IT

In Italy, Germany, France and England, where most of the Jews lived, whole communities were frequently attacked. Men, women, and children were killed or wounded; houses were burnt and property was destroyed. Jews were forced to wear special badges and, in some cities, had to live in separate districts which later became known as ghettos. At times, rulers protected the Jews, if they were paid large sums of money to do so. After a while, these rulers began to look upon Jews as if they were a mine from which gold and silver could be gotten at all times.

When a king found that the Jews in his land were poor and no more money could be squeezed out of them, he drove them out of his country. That is what happened in England in 1290, and in France in 1394. It did not happen in Germany and Italy because they were then divided into small states. When the Jews were driven out of one state, they went to live in another.

It was not so in Spain. The Jews in every community had an organization which governed them. They collected their own taxes, paying part to the government and keeping the rest for their own needs. They judged their wrong-doers in their own courts, held in the synagogues. When a Jew took a Christian to court, the case was tried before Jewish and Christian judges so as to make sure that both the Jew and the Christian would be fairly treated.

The Jews of Spain earned their living in many different ways. Some were landowners. These either rented their land to others or hired men to farm it. Many owned small pieces of land, and earned a living by farming. Others were hand-workers: that is, shoemakers, weavers, dyers, smiths, bookbinders, or watchmakers. Still others were storekeepers or clerks. Only a small number of Spanish Jews earned a living, as they did in France or Germany, by making loans at interest. Life in Spain was, therefore, far more pleasant for the Jews than it was in other European lands.

However, the Christian leaders at that time wanted the Jews to be continually annoyed so that they would finally give up their religion and become Christians. They therefore urged the king to carry out the Pope's orders to separate Jews from Christians and make life hard and unpleasant for them. When the king refused, some clever priests tried a different plan to make the Spanish Jews give up their religion.

They asked the king to arrange a debate between them and the rabbis in order to prove to the Jews that Chistianity was a better religion. The king did as the priests asked, and commanded the Jews to choose a learned rabbi to debate with the priests. The man they chose was Rabbi Moses Nachmanides.

Answer the questions to Topic I on Chapter 24.

II. WHY NACHMANIDES WAS CHOSEN SPOKESMAN

Who was Rabbi Nachmanides? Why was he chosen to speak in the name of the Spanish Jews? Nachmanides was born some 750 years ago of a family of well-known rabbis. From his early boyhood, he had studied Torah, Talmud, and medicine. When he grew up, he became a doctor, but spent most of his time studying the Talmud. In fact, he wrote a book about the Talmud when he was only fifteen years old.

Nachmanides became known for his love both of God and of his fellow-Jews. Unlike Maimonides, *he did not figure out why people should obey the laws of the Torah.* He simply believed that everything in the Torah was not only true, but holy. To him, it seemed that the Torah contained all the knowledge that a person needed to have, and that anyone who really understood the Torah could find out all the secrets about God, the Messiah, the world to come, and everything else that he might want to know. It was his opinion that people did not know these great secrets only because they had not studied the Torah in the right way. And so, he spent all his free time studying the Torah and the explanations of it found in the Talmud, or the works of great rabbis who lived before him.

When Nachmanides became known as a great scholar, he did not become proud. On the contrary! He continued to have the deepest respect for the learned rabbis who had lived before his time. In fact, he considered their words almost as holy as the words of the Torah, and studied them with care.

Nachmanides even respected Maimonides in spite of the fact that he disagreed with some of his ideas. In fact, he wrote a little book defending Maimonides at the time when many people were trying to show that the great thinker was not a good Jew. Nachmanides must certainly have been a very gentle as well as a learned man.

Answer the questions to Topic II.

III. RABBI VS. PRIEST IN DEBATING

The Jews were wise in choosing a gentle as well as a learned scholar to speak for them. Emphatic words against the Christian religion could only have brought trouble to them all.

The debate was held in the palace of the Spanish king. A great many priests, high officials of the king, and the king himself were present. A small number

The debate was held in the palace. . . .

of Jews were also admitted. Nachmanides was very careful to say nothing against the Christian religion, even though the king himself told him that he could say anything he wished, without fear of punishment. The rabbi simply explained why Jews did not believe in Christianity. He pointed out that the Jews could not believe that Jesus was a Messiah, because there were many wars still going on, whereas, according to the prophets, during the days of the Messiah there would be only peace.

The debate lasted for three days. When it was over, the king gave Nachmanides a fine present to show how pleased he was with his words. The Jews rejoiced greatly. They had expected trouble and were glad that none came. But some of the priests were angry because a Jew had won the debate, and said that Nachmanides had lost. The rabbi then published the speeches he had made. The priests immediately brought the book to the king and said that in it Nachmanides had been disrespectful to the Christian religion. The king then ordered that the rabbi be sent out of Spain. The fact that Nachmanides was an old man of more than seventy years did not change the king's mind. The plea that the king had promised not to hurt him for what he might say, did not help. Nothing helped. Nachmanides was forced to leave Spain when he was old and gray and feeble. This was the first sign of the trouble that was soon to come upon the Jews of Spain.

Answer the questions to Topic III.

IV. THE TEACHINGS OF NACHMANIDES

This time, the unfair decision had not seriously hurt the Jews. No one but Nachmanides suffered. Even the rabbi himself was rather glad to follow the steps of Judah Halevi and Maimonides and to go to the land of his fathers—Palestine, as they had done. When he arrived, however, Nachmanides was greatly disappointed in what he saw. Palestine was again in the hands of the Mohammedans. The land was in ruins because of the many wars which had taken place in it. Jerusalem was almost deserted. Only broken-down houses and complete ruins were to be seen in the city streets. So deserted was the city that land could be gotten for almost nothing, and yet no people came to take possession of it. Nachmanides was unable to find even ten Jewish men living in the city.

Nevertheless, Nachmanides settled in Jerusalem and busied himself with writing an explanation of the Torah. In this book, he tried to explain what he considered to be the real meanings of some of the Bible stories. The stories about Isaac and Ishmael, he thought, foretold troubles which Jews would suffer at the hands of Mohammedans. The stories about Jacob and Esau seemed to Nachmanides to refer to hardships which Rome would cause the Jews. Nachmanides also figured out the date on which he expected the Messiah to come. And many Jews living at that time thought he was right, and actually awaited the Messiah.

The years passed slowly, but no Messiah came to save the people. Instead, they suffered more than ever before. In Germany, Italy, and France, the officers were very strict in forcing Jews to live in special sections, wear yellow badges, keep away from Christians, and earn their living by dealing in second-hand goods or money lending. At times, Jews were attacked by mobs who beat, robbed, and even murdered them. Yet the Jews did not lose hope. Many a rabbi spent his days and nights searching holy books in an effort to find the date of the Messiah's coming, while the people confidently awaited his early arrival.

And yet, the Jews were not altogether unhappy. Even in the German cities, where they were most harshly treated, they were not always sad. On Sabbaths and holidays, they dresssed in their best and went to the synagogue for services. When the prayers were over, they returned home and ate a hearty meal. They then spent the rest of the day amusing themselves. They loved to ask riddles, play chess, indulge in games with nuts, dance, talk, and study Bible, Talmud, and other holy books.

In Spain, they were of course much happier. There they governed themselves, lived in the finest districts, held high offices, and rarely suffered from attacks by their Christian neighbors.

And so we find that even though the Jews, particularly outside of Spain, were unfairly treated by the kings, princes, and priests, looked down upon by their neighbors, hated by the merchants who considered them competitors, and often attacked by cruel people, they had the courage to live on. Their faith in God even made it possible for them to enjoy life, and look hopefully to a time when the Messiah would finally come and bring happiness to all.

Answer the questions to Topic IV.

ADDITIONAL READING

The Great March. The story of the debate is told in "The Rabbi Wins," on pages 184–190.

Great Men in Israel. "The Jew Speaks," tells about the rabbi and the priest. The story is found on pages 100–104.

An example of the sufferings of Jews in Germany hundreds of years back is told in "The Rabbi in the Prison Tower," on pages 105–109.

Great Jews since Bible Times. Read "How Nachmanides Found the Palace of the King," beginning on page 79.

SOMETHING TO THINK ABOUT

1. Debates such as those in which Nachmanides took part occurred rather frequently. Can you tell why Jews disliked to take part in such debates?
2. Why did Jews so eagerly and so confidently expect the arrival of the Messiah?

They had the courage to live on.

What Happened to the Jews in Spain?

FOR 450 years, beginning with the time when Hasdai helped his fellow-Jews build a center for Judaism in Spain, a thousand years ago, up to 550 years ago, our people lived happily in that land. Popes and priests tried but did not succeed in persuading the kings or the people to treat the Jews harshly. Only rarely were they attacked. It happened in the days of Maimonides, but the laws against the Jews were not enforced for very long. Nachmanides was forced to leave Spain; but he alone suffered, while the Jewish people were not otherwise hurt.

There were two reasons why the Jews of Spain were well treated. (1) They were needed in Spain. The Christians wanted their help and money for driving out the Mohammedans, while the Mohammedans wanted them to help fight the Christians. (2) The kings had found that the Jews were good citizens and were fair enough to protect them.

I. HOW MARRANOS CAME INTO BEING

About 550 years ago, things began to change in Spain. By that time the Christians had succeeded in winning almost all of Spain. There was very little danger that the Mohammedans would ever get it back. Jews were, therefore, no longer as necessary as before. The kings then began to tax them unfairly. These taxes were so high that, in one city, the Jews had to sell the ornaments on their Sifre Torah (Scrolls of the Law) in order to get the money which the king demanded from them.

The unfriendliness of the king was quickly noted by some evil priests. One fiery priest urged the people to attack and kill all the Jews. At his suggestion the people fell upon the Jews living in Seville. Thousands of them were killed; the others escaped death by giving up their religion and becoming Christians.

The people in other Spanish cities followed the example set in Seville. They robbed, wounded, and murdered the Jews or dragged them off to church to be converted to Christianity. When peace was finally restored, the number of Jews in Spain had been cut almost in half. Many thousands had been killed and many more thousands had become Christians in order to save their lives and their homes.

The new Christians did not expect to remain Christians for long, and secretly observed the laws of Judaism. They were therefore disliked by the other Christians. The Jews, on the other hand, also disliked them for having given up their own religion. Thus they became known by the Spanish name "Marranos," which means the "Accursed Ones."

Answer the questions to Topic I of Chapter 25.

Nachmanides was forced to leave Spain; . . .

II. HOW THE NUMBER OF MARRANOS INCREASED

Christian leaders were happy because they had succeeded in bringing so many of our people to the church. But they were not yet satisfied. They urged the king to enforce all the laws issued by the Popes against the Jews. To this, the king finally agreed, about 500 years ago. Spanish Jews were then forced to live by themselves in special parts of the cities, known as Juderias. They were compelled to wear yellow badges on their outer garments. They were dismissed from all government positions, and they lost the right to try Jewish wrong-doers in their own courts. Many Jews found life under the new conditions so disagreeable, that they gave up their religion and joined the Marranos.

Zealous priests now proceeded with their plans to make Christians of all the remaining Jews. With the king's permission, they began to preach in the synagogues, while soldiers forced the Jews to listen. They succeeded in winning over many Jews, not by proving that Christianity was better, but by showing how miserable they could make the life of a Jew. They also arranged debates like the one in which Nachmanides had taken part, and brought many more Jews to the Christian church.

Thus the number of Marranos grew and grew. Jews who desired to hold government positions became Christians. Those who did not want to live in the Juderias gave up their religion. Those who wanted to be respected by Christians ceased being Jews. In fact all who were not strong enough to bear suffering, left Judaism and accepted the Christian religion.

Answer the questions to Topic II.

III. WHY THE INQUISITION WAS ESTABLISHED

As might be expected, most of the Marranos had a greater love for Judaism than for Christianity. Secretly, they kept the Jewish holidays, taught their children Torah, and at the first opportunity, returned to their religion. To put a stop to these practices, a special court, called the Inquisition, was created. Its purpose was to find out which Christians were not faithful to their religion, and to punish them.

Most of the officers and judges of the Inquisition were hard-hearted and cruel men. If they suspected a Christian of being faithless to his religion, they immediately threw him into a deep dark prison. If the victim refused to admit that he had sinned, the officers of the Inquisition tortured him cruelly. To escape the terrible pain, most people admitted anything the officers wanted. The poor fellows were then burnt alive, and their property went to the king's treasury.

Thousands of Marranos were arrested and hundreds of them were burnt or left to die in prison. Every Marrano lived in constant terror of being imprisoned by officers of the Inquisition. He feared to buy Mazzot or Maror (bitter-herb) for Pesach. He was afraid not to kindle a fire on the Sabbath. He did not dare to cover his table with a fresh tablecloth on a Jewish festival, lest he be reported to the Inquisition. As for kindling the candles on the eve of Sabbath or a festival, the Marranos did not even dare *think* of doing it.

Answer the questions to Topic III.

IV. DID THE INQUISITION MAKE LOYAL CHRISTIANS OF THE MARRANOS?

And yet both Jews and Marranos lived on in Spain. Indeed, many were fairly happy. Large numbers of Jews stilled owned land and possessed great wealth. Most of them were still able to earn a living in one way or another. They still had beautiful synagogues and excellent schools, and generally their neighbors treated them in a friendly manner.

There is another reason why Jews found it pleasant to stay in Spain—the officers were not very strict in enforcing the laws against the Jews. Many of them never lived in the Juderias, never wore yellow badges and always kept in close touch with their Christian neighbors. Indeed, the king himself employed the Jew, Isaac Abrabanel, as his treasurer, despite the law against using Jews as officers of the government.

Here is how it happened. The Christian king of Spain was carrying on a war against the Mohammedans, and needed large sums of money. He therefore decided to get a good treasurer. He learned that Abrabanel had taken care of the treasury for the king of Portugal and had done his work well. Reports on the honesty of Abrabanel also pleased the king. And so he appointed him to this high office. Abrabanel proved to be a good choice. He raised large sums of money for the king and was able to supply him with all he needed. Naturally, the king was highly pleased and befriended his Jewish treasurer. He often asked for his advice on important matters and, from time to time, the king showed kindness to the Jews, at the special request of Abrabanel.

Thus the Jews lived in Spain more happily than in other European lands. Marranos were always able to learn from them when Jewish holidays were to be celebrated and how they might be observed. And despite all the dangers of the Inquisition, they remained more loyal to Judaism than to Christianity.

Answer the questions to Topic IV.

V. WHAT FINALLY HAPPENED TO THE JEWS OF SPAIN

The Spanish people finally realized that they could never make true Christians out of the Marranos unless they could prevent them from meeting with Jews. There was only one way to do this—drive all the Jews from Spain. The queen, in her eagerness to make Spain a purely Christian land, finally convinced the king to do this terrible thing. With the money which his Jewish treasurer, Abrabanel, raised for him, the king succeeded in destroying the last little Mohammedan kingdom, in 1492. *He and his queen then celebrated the victory by ordering all Jews and Mohammedans to leave Spain within four months.*

Abrabanel pleaded with the king to take back his unjust command. He offered him large sums of money to allow the Jews to remain. But the king insisted. On Tisha b'Ab, the very day on which the Temple had been destroyed 1422 years earlier, the Jews sorrowfully left the land in which they and their ancestors had lived for over a thousand years.

The Jews now scattered more widely than ever. Many went to North Africa. Large numbers of Jews settled in Turkey. Some went to Italy, and others found their way to Poland and Lithuania and elsewhere in eastern Europe.

Their life there was very unpleasant. In most places they were unwelcome strangers. But the Jewish people somehow escaped destruction. How the Jews overcame their hardships, won their freedom, regained their self-respect, and enriched their life with literature, music, and art is a long and interesting story. It will be told in your next volume on Jewish History.

Answer the questions to Topic V.

ADDITIONAL READING

The Great March. "Whither-Now?" beginning on page 222 tells of the exile of the Jews from Spain. Read the story.

Great Men in Israel. "With a Song on Their Lips," pages 110–114, is another retelling of the story of the Spanish Exile. Read it.

Great Jews since Bible Times. "A Friend at Court," pages 83–86, tells about Isaac Abrabanel. "The Wandering People," pages 88–90 repeats the sad tale of how the Jews were forced to leave Spain.

The Jews now scattered more widely than ever.

SOMETHING TO THINK ABOUT

1. What led the king of Spain to order all Jews to leave Spain?
2. Why did both Jews and Christians dislike the Marranos?
3. In the face of all the hardships, Jews lived on and enjoyed life. What made it possible for them to do so?

Index

L

M

N

T